At Home in Creativity
The Naturalistic Theology
of Henry Nelson Wieman

Bruce Southworth

SKINNER HOUSE BOOKS
BOSTON

Published by Skinner House Books,
an imprint of the
Unitarian Universalist Association,
25 Beacon Street, Boston, MA 02108-2800.

Printed in Canada.

ISBN 1-55896-297-2

10 9 8 7 6 5 4 3 2 1
99 98 97 96 95

CONTENTS

Take the need simply to feel at home in the world. It is a primary spiritual and moral need. Some otherworldly approaches to religion may suggest that our true home is elsewhere. But prophetic and pragmatic religion argues otherwise. It insists, in the words of feminist theologian Nelle Morton, that "the journey *is* home."

William Sloane Coffin puts it this way: "The chief religious question can no longer be, 'What am I going to do to be saved?' It must be, 'What are we all going to do together, to save God's creation?'"

All proposed solutions are perspectival, yet underlying them all is an undeniable reality. There is a unity in which all five and a half billion of us now on this planet are all involved. A unity, universal and eternal. It is not a unity that we humans are called on to create. No, it is given. The religious and reflective task is to become more aware of this reality, then to embrace it more gratefully and make it more manifest in the choices we make and the lives we lead, no matter how we name that unity—or choose not to name it at all.

We Unitarian Universalists, who carry in our very name a call to make that unity clearer, are a diverse group ourselves. We differ in worship, theology, politics, background, and perspective. We are drawn together by something akin to a method of religious inquiry.

The philosopher Henry Nelson Wieman, who in his later years made his home with us, called this method "creative interchange." We also share a practical desire to make a difference in the world. When I preside at a wedding or service of union, or dedicate a new home for a family or for a religious community, I often give this prayer of blessing:

> May the home that you make together be of the kind that helps to make this world a bit more homelike. May it be a place of virtue and of honor, of hospitality and of peace, where all who come in peace are welcomed, and where the young are wisely nurtured. Above all, may you find such fulfillment [t]here that you never cease to reach out in love and concern for others, so that those who follow your lives will have cause to rejoice not only in your happiness, but in your brave and generous living.

Wieman taught, without supernaturalism, that our success depends on more than ethics. You may try to be my friend, for example. I may try to be yours. Both of us may treat one another well. We can set the necessary but not sufficient conditions for friendship to grow. But we cannot guarantee it. The source of any new value, of any human good, is always a "creative event" that we cannot completely control, marked by something akin to grace.

A mentor of mine once studied Wieman's thought. He concluded that since "creative events" occur in many different forms, polytheism is superior to any form of monotheism. Impressed with this insight, he found an occasion to preach a sermon on the theme to the Unitarian Fellowship of Carbondale, IL, where Wieman, then in his eighties, was a member.

The philosopher listened attentively. At the conclusion of the service, he shook hands with the speaker. "My friend," he suggested, "you and I need *much more* creative interchange!"

Religious liberals today share that need for more creative interchange. So does the world. We need to go beyond polite pluralism and also beyond our many differences in rhetoric, in worship, tradition, and perception.

At the close of his book, *The Unitarians and the Universalists*, historian David Robinson issues a challenge. He points out that in every previous generation, our religious tradition has helped American culture to assimilate some new, much-needed philosophical insight. In Channing's era, it was so-called "common sense" philosophy and Lockean empiricism. In Emerson's, it was the transcendentalism of Kant, the moral imperative that challenged slavery and the oppression of women. In the late nineteenth century, it was creation as evolution, and in the early twentieth, the democratic pragmatism of John Dewey's educational humanism.

But recently, Robinson suggests, both we and our culture have been so busy with pragmatic involvement and the rhetorics thereof that we have neglected philosophical reflection. "Process thought," as pioneered by Whitehead, popularized and pragmatized by Wieman, and refined by Hartshorne, deserves far more "creative interchange" among us, so that its spirit might help the whole culture to consider both the programs and the processes needed to preserve a home in creation and in creativity for the human spirit itself.

This introduction to the naturalistic theology of Henry Nelson Wieman, so ably prepared by Bruce Southworth, is a fine contribution to renewing creative, philosophical interchange among us. As in all good and hospitable homes, may you find yourself so at home in these pages that you are inspired to speak and act with more creativity than before.

John A. Buehrens, President
Unitarian Universalist Association

❧

INTRODUCTION

There are many brilliant and creative contemporary liberal theologies in North America, and they come in many flavors and moods. But something is missing from many of the best.

Liberation, feminist, creation-centered, and scientific theologies, to name several of the possible major groupings, offer refreshing and vivifying perspectives. They often share, despite their diverse appreciations and symbols, unifying themes in their common concern for both personal transformation and social liberation. They also often reflect a contextual (rather than a deductive) method that honors the experiences of specific communities of faith and action.

In addition, many represent new expressions of the empirical, pragmatic, and prophetic currents that have long been a distinctive element of American theology. Nevertheless, frequently missing is an appreciation for the intellectual foundations of faith as historically pursued through the philosophy of religion.

For many, this omission is a positive step away from old, oppressive ideologies/theologies. For others, the practical matters of worship and devotional practice as well as social analysis and critique receive primary emphasis.

For these and other reasons, intellectual rigor in articulating religious faith, once the hallmark of twentieth century American theology, has receded. One risk is that theology is reduced to personal psychology and/or social ethics if the fundamental philosophical issues are skirted. To be sure, some of the rationalist currents of theology by their abstruse language and/or their lack of interest in worship have, intentionally or not, divorced themselves from popular faith and practice.

This study addresses some of the intellectual requisites of faith that are often neglected today, and in doing so I turn to the philosophy of religion of Henry Nelson Wieman. For me, Wieman's philosophy of religion and empirical theology offer useful tools for understanding a variety of contemporary liberal theologies and for articulating deeper faith for our times.

Wieman's career first blossomed during the 1920s and 1930s when Karl Barth, continental theology, and neo-orthodoxy were ascending. Liberals for a brief time confidently held their ground. Charles Clayton Morrison, editor of the *Christian Century*, spoke for many when he declared, "I don't need Barth! Wieman is my Barth!"[1]

For many liberals, Henry Nelson Wieman (1884-1975) as a philosopher of religion "saved" theology from the conservative Barthians (and with theology also saved religious faith and practice). At the same time, because he advocated a vigorous theism, he took issue with those who embraced humanism. Wieman thus gave substantial aid and comfort to liberal Christianity from the attacks on it from both the right and the left.

Creative, brilliant, and faithful to his mystical inspiration, Henry Nelson Wieman made a distinctive contribution to American theology as a philosopher of religion. He embraced the modernist spirit and believed that scientific inquiry was an appropriate and a necessary method for both theological discourse and revitalized religious practice.

Wieman's primary contribution was to offer new ways to speak intelligibly about God. At a time when dualistic supernaturalism was resurgent, Wieman countered with a naturalistic alternative that was distinctly American in character.

The nature of God, and especially God's love, was subject to grand theological debate in the 1920s and 1930s. This debate intensified after World War II because of that war's unique horrors. Wieman's formulations about God responded to the issues of his times and took mature form in *The Source Of Human Good,* published in 1946.

For Wieman, God was not a philosophical proposition to be proved or disproved. God is a given, a datum of reality. More precisely in Wieman's language, God is an event, a Creative Event, an event of Creative Interchange. God is Creativity. As such, God is trustworthy, reliable, and sustaining. God is that which can transform and save humans in ways in which we cannot transform ourselves, provided that we understand and fulfill the requisite conditions.

From his position at the University of Chicago Divinity School as Professor of Christian Theology (and later as Professor of Philosophy of Religion) and during an active "retirement" at other universities (primarily at Southern Illinois University), Wieman influenced not only the course of liberal theology in the United States, but also and especially Unitarian Universalist theology. Ordained a Presbyterian minister in 1912, he received ministerial fellowship as a Unitarian in 1949.

Today, his contributions are not so apparent. Wieman, who was liberal Christianity's answer to Barth and to humanism sixty years ago, is seldom, if ever, mentioned with the preliberationist constellation of theological stars of this century: Karl Barth, Alfred North Whitehead, Reinhold Niebuhr, and Paul Tillich.

As influential as Wieman was during the middle third of this century, liberal theology took other paths away from a strict empiricism. Some, like Charles Hartshorne, pursued a rational empiricism with an elaborate process metaphysics built upon the thought of Alfred North Whitehead. Others, like Paul Van Buren and Gabriel Vahanian, moved toward linguistic analysis and logical positivism that culminated in the "death of God" movement of the 1960s. Over the past twenty years, liberation theologies (African American, Latin American, feminist, Creation-centered, and others) have emerged.

More recently, in the last decade a modest revival of empirical theology has begun with notable contributions appearing in the *American Journal of Theology and Phi-*

losophy and in the SUNY Series in Religious Studies, to name but two streams. This particular study seeks to contribute to that revival and will outline Wieman's thought, his contribution to American theology, and the continuing relevance of his philosophy of religion. Embedded within that philosophy of religion are a theological method and doctrines that remain useful to liberal religionists today. It is of special interest that contemporary liberation theologies reflect significant points of common concern, although rarely any direct continuity, with Wieman's theology.

Within Wieman's thought are resources for a revitalized liberal theology, particularly when his ideas are expanded and applied beyond the scope of his primary agenda regarding conceptual clarity about God. Cornel West writes of the urgent need for a "prophetic pragmatism," and Wieman's thought can contribute to that formidable task.[2]

Can a white, Anglo-European, classically trained, male philosopher of religion of a prior generation still offer insights into God's presence and human action in the world? I believe so.

◆ ◆ ◆

The empirical theology of Henry Nelson Wieman has offered me the initial intellectual foundation for a sustaining, liberating, and transforming faith. Like Wieman, I resonate with the need in our modern age for clear, naturalistic concepts about God and share the conviction that an empirical method is essential.

During my studies at Union Theological Seminary, I read

Wieman's work eagerly and began to outline the theological doctrines implicit in his philosophy of religion. To my surprise, such a treatment had not yet appeared,[3] and I received encouragement for the task from Professors J. A. Martin of Columbia University and James Bergland of Union Theological Seminary.

During eighteen years of parish ministry, I have continued to find intellectual nourishment and spiritual challenge from Wieman's thought and from a wide assortment of contemporary liberal and liberation theologies. The common themes and threads have prompted this study in historical theology, which I believe adds substance to many of the more recent theologies. Among those who have contributed to my further understanding of Wieman and of contemporary currents are Diane Arakawa, John Buehrens, William Minor, Peter Paris, Creighton Peden, Sid Peterman, Tracey Robinson-Harris, James Washington, and Clarke Wells.

Theology must serve daily religious living if it is to be of value, and I continue to find Wieman's description of the sacred in "creative interchange" and of God in "creativity" to be illuminating, empowering, and spiritually challenging. The significance of his theology for daily religious living is apparent to me in my own life, and I take those matters up in a separate, companion volume of sermons, *Meeting God—Sermons in the Spirit of Henry Nelson Wieman.*

My goal here is historical and constructive: to introduce the thought of Henry Nelson Wieman, who offers liberal religionists a potent legacy.

CHAPTER ONE

Biographical Sketch

"The one thing needful is to enjoy the visitor when she or he is present with us, whether one comes in the form of a sunset, or tall tree, or a singing bird, or a child tugging at our hand, or a pleasant fire on a winter evening, or what not."

Henry Nelson Wieman, as a philosopher of religion and as an empirical theologian, focused on one central problem throughout his career as a thinker, teacher, and scholar. In his "Intellectual Autobiography," he states in the form of a question the problem that engaged his attention for over fifty years:

> What operates in human life with such character and power that it will transform men and women as they cannot transform themselves, saving them from evil and leading them to the best that human life can ever reach, provided they meet the required conditions?[1]

Wieman's religious concern for human salvation has characterized his eighteen books and numerous articles.[2]

Regarding the "required conditions," a primary one for Wieman is religious faith, by which he means a total commitment of the self to creativity.[3]

Wieman formulated his mature answer to the problem that he so steadfastly pursued in terms of the saving and transforming power of the process of creativity that operates in human lives. Wieman most often discusses this general process of creativity in terms of concrete instances of "creative events," "creative communication," and "creative interchange." Creativity is "the ultimate category" and is to be used "hypothetically and experimentally for wise guidance in human behavior."[4] Although he first describes the fourfold character of creative events in *The Source of Human Good* (1946), his discussions of communication, growth, and the increase of connective meaning in his earlier works indicate a continuity of thought throughout his career.

Wieman identifies a Creative Event as God. It is God that operates in human lives saving and transforming us in ways beyond our own abilities alone. It is the conditions of God's-Creativity that we must meet. Religious living thus means adjusting ourselves to God-Creativity.

To summarize: Wieman's philosophical and theological goal responded to the question, "How do we know/experience God?"

The answer: In Creativity.

Simultaneously, he was asking, "How might we be saved?"

The answer: By faith—by ultimate commitment to God, which is commitment to the Creative Process, a commitment that necessitates our co-creativity.

Early Years: The Interpersonal and the Mystical

Henry Nelson Wieman was born on August 19, 1884 in Rich Hill, Missouri. His mother was an important influence in his life, and he writes about their relationship:

> When I was a boy we had long intimate talks in which each tried to express to the other what either most deeply felt and thought. We did not talk about religion particularly, but about anything which at the time seemed to be of chief concern. I would come from those talks with a feeling of exultation, release and aspiration, as though there was something great to live for.[5]

Such moments of creative communication, or creative interchange, are ones in which new meaning and value emerges. Such experiences would became paradigmatic for Wieman. This concern and profound appreciation for the interpersonal and its power appear in one of his earliest books, *Methods of Private Religious Living*. For Wieman, intimate communication reflects one of the highest forms of mystical experience:

> Consider an . . . example of this kind of mystical experience....
>
>   Tom and Dick are out for a walk. They are old friends. They do not talk. They understand one another and so there is nothing to talk about. But they are deeply and richly conscious of the fact that they are together. Their togetherness is the thing that is

happening to them in the immediate present and of
which they are appreciatively conscious. It fills them
with a deep feeling of contentment. Such experience
of friendship not only integrates each personality in
itself, but involves discernment of an organic unity
which includes both the individuals as well as the
autumn leaves, the haze that hangs over the trees,
the trees themselves, the sky, and unfathomed depths
of experience. Is the integrating movement of the
universe excluded from such an experience? We do
not see how it can be.[6]

Wieman comments, "In the mystic experience we now
have before us, the integration of the personality of the
subject is incidental to ... discernment of a much wider integration, far exceeding the bounds ... of personality, but
to which one can unite oneself as one organic member."[7]

Such an experience of interpersonally inspired transcendence is a holy, sacred moment, a moment of grace. Wieman
would later draw on the work of Harry Stack Sullivan (*The
Interpersonal Theory of Psychiatry*), and he equated such
I-Thou moments—moments of creative interchange—
with God's presence and grace.[8]

Those early, holy moments in intense conversation with
his mother remained with him. As a teacher he was re-
nowned for the kindness and character of classroom and
personal discussions. He practiced what he taught. These
experiences were a living part of his religion.

About his upbringing, Wieman also writes, "I was never

taught religion. But I caught something from my parents by contagion. In time it formulated itself into a religion."[9]

Again, note the interpersonal dimension in its vivacious contagion. He continues, "I was never led to feel that religion was identified with the church. We all went to church, more or less. But, being the oldest in a family of eight children, I often remained at home to take care of the baby. The baby almost always slept and I read poetry—Tennyson, Byron, and at an earlier age, Longfellow. I remember still the inspiration of those Sunday morning poems. The poems were not religious...."[10]

And yet the experience was. Once again it is the primacy of the "felt quality" of such experiences to which Wieman always sought to be faithful. Our experience is far richer than we can describe, analyze, or categorize; and appreciative awareness of that fact characterizes Wieman's theology.

Personal theology is inevitably shaped by autobiography, and a clue to Wieman's later thoughts about the church emerges when he reports, "The business of keeping the church going is the most religious religion there is. But it was never the religion of my mother and father, although he was a clergyman."[11]

For Wieman, the institutional church is profoundly important, but it could not be equated with or overshadow the personal, religious experience of transformation. Although his career revolved around the philosophical task of conceptual clarity and analysis of what empirically shapes and can transform us, mystical appreciation remained an essential element of Wieman's life. To understand Wieman, it is important always to keep in mind his ultimate sensuality—his focus on the rich, deeply felt quality of immediate experience.

Methods of Private Religious Living, first published in 1929, went through five reprintings in the subsequent decade, and its discussion of mysticism is insightful. In it he distinguishes among eleven kinds of mystical experience, only two of which he believes to be truly healthy, life-giving, and transforming. And this brilliantly intellectual philosopher of religion writes about the limits of human reason in coming to any knowledge of God:

> The cosmic process in which and with which we live, when we live well, far exceeds any powers of comprehension we have thus far achieved. All our ideas are inadequate for making adjustment to it. Hence we must ever strive for more inclusive integrations in dealing with it. To this end we must periodically turn aside from our routine activities and sit in mystic quietude in order that more adequate insights may come to us. In this way we are able to pierce more deeply into the mystery that encompasses us, explore the unexplored, and imagine the unimagined. This is the great task of religion. It is the way we learn to live more intimately with God.[12]

In his "Intellectual Autobiography," Wieman describes a transforming experience as a senior at Park College. At this explicitly Christian college he had been impressed by Ernest McAfee, who taught comparative religion, and by

Silas Evans, who taught philosophy. Nonetheless, throughout most of his college years, as during high school, he had been contemplating a career in journalism. On an April evening, however, he reports, rather tersely, "I came to my room after the evening meal and sat alone looking at the sunset over the Missouri River. Suddenly it came over me that I should devote my life to the problems of religious inquiry. I never had a more ecstatic experience. I could not sleep all night and walked in that ecstasy for days."[13]

With this new direction, Wieman enrolled at San Francisco Seminary (Presbyterian) not so much to prepare for parish ministry as to pursue "the religious problem." Having received a fellowship upon graduation, he went to Jena and Heidelberg in Germany for a year of study in 1910-1911.

For four years he served a Presbyterian Church in Davis, California, with the hope of establishing an effective campus ministry. During that time, his interest in further study and teaching only increased. He also concluded that for him to reach students he would do better by being directly involved in their education as a teacher.

Early Academic Career

In 1915, Wieman entered the doctoral program in the Philosophy Department at Harvard University, not at the Divinity School. He studied with William Ernest Hocking and Ralph Barton Perry among others and earned his Ph.D. in 1917. The genesis of Wieman's philosophy of creativity appears in his dissertation "The Organization of Interests" and reflects the influence of (1) Ralph Barton Perry's interest theory of value, empiricism, and epistemological realism; (2) William Ernest Hocking's philosophy of absolute idealism (although Wieman rejects it) and concern for interpersonal creativity; (3) Josiah Royce's theory of interpretation and sense of life as a cosmic, prophetic adventure; (4) Henri Bergson's philosophy of creativity; and (5) William James's and John Dewey's instrumentalism, empiricism, and pragmatism.[14]

Wieman wrestled with each of these thinkers and others over the years and shaped his own distinctive position that was value-centered, empirical, naturalistic, pragmatic, and soteriological.

From 1917 to 1927, Wieman taught philosophy of religion and theology at Occidental College. His first book in 1926, *Religious Experience and Scientific Method* (published in 1926), with its clarity of thought and expression along with an endorsement from Dewey, captured the attention of liberal academic colleagues.

At that time, religious orthodoxy with its supernaturalism was no longer tenable or creditable for many in academia. One alternative included religious humanism, which embraced a naturalistic, scientific worldview. Another included a continuing focus on biblical criticism and to some extent on the search for the historical Jesus, a project that was becoming increasingly difficult to sustain.

A pressing problem was emerging. Religious experience, worship, and religious habits clearly remained a part of human experience, but God was a problem: How do we talk about God in meaningful ways in a modern age? Does

God exist as an objective reality? Can theology affirm that "God is as good as Jesus?"

To this problem, Wieman responded with brilliance. "If Henry Nelson Wieman's contribution had been limited to this one publication (*Religious Experience and Scientific Method*), his place still would have been secure in the field of constructive theology in American religious thought."[15] Such is the evaluation of Creighton Peden and Larry Axel in their essay concluding *Creative Freedom*, a volume of Wieman's writings that they edited after his death.

Wieman offered for consideration this assertion, which liberals welcomed: "Whatever the word God may mean, it is a term used to designate that Something upon which human life is most dependent for its security, welfare and increasing abundance. That there is such a Something cannot be doubted. The mere fact that human life happens, and continues to happen, proves that this Something, however unknown, does certainly exist."[16]

The issue about God's existence, he asserted, was the wrong question. The proper question is one of theological method, the means by which we come to learn about God. He went on to describe this method as one akin to the empirical method of science with hypothesizing, testing, evaluating, and correcting one's ideas and knowledge of God.

Wieman, in opposition to philosophical idealism, was reaffirming the sovereignty of God, just as Karl Barth and Reinhold Niebuhr were. But unlike the orthodox or neo-orthodox, his method embraced rationalism and empiricism along with a philosophy of organism influenced by Alfred North Whitehead's *Concept of Nature*.[17] Wieman's familiarity with and understanding of Whitehead significantly advanced greater appreciation of Whitehead's innovative synthesis.

About this particular book, Wieman would write: "When Whitehead's *The Concept of Nature* appeared it fascinated me. One blistering hot and stupefying summer in Southern California I toiled for many days upon it. Strange how one can detect the greatness of a man's thought before everyone can fathom it and even before the thinker himself has developed the implications of it or rounded it out."[18]

Chicago

With this major work published and acclaimed, Wieman served as a visiting professor at the Divinity School of the University of Chicago during the summer of 1926. Then in 1927 he joined the faculty where he was to serve as Professor of Christian Theology and later as Professor of Philosophy. Bernard Meland, who was to collaborate with Wieman on *American Philosophies of Religion* and to become a colleague at Chicago, writes about the excitement that Wieman's presence generated. "The initial impact of Wieman's coming to Chicago was one of expectancy and hope. The freshness of Wieman's language and his manner of addressing inquiries seemed to break through much of the ennui that had settled over well-worn explications within the modernist mode of empiricism. This is what gave zest and a note of expectancy to what Wieman offered in the classroom or in faculty discussion and in his writing as well."[19]

Wieman's reputation preceded him not only because of *Religious Experience and Scientific Method* and his summer quarter of teaching, but also because of his performance at a meeting of the Theology Club during the fall of 1926 when he was teaching at McCormick Seminary as a visiting professor.

Alfred North Whitehead's *Religion in the Making* had appeared and was creating a sensation. Bernard Meland reports,

> ... to the dismay and irritation of many who were then with the Divinity School of the University of Chicago, including such students of the history and development of religious doctrine and institutions as Shailer Mathews, Edward Scribner Ames, and Shirley Jackson Case, this book was wholly unintelligible.... The occasion of Wieman's interpretation was a meeting of the Theology Club of the Divinity School in the Swift Common Room. Edward Scribner Ames, Shirley Jackson Case, Gerald Birney Smith, Shailer Mathews, and their colleagues were all there, most of them in the front row, and behind them a packed audience extended to the rear of the room, all awaiting the miracle of interpreting "this book." The miracle was performed. With deftness and patience, and with occasional sallies in poetic imagination, Wieman took the key phrases and their basic concepts and translated them into the more familiar imagery of the pragmatic Chicago School. It was as if shuttered windows in one's own household had been

swung open, revealing vistas of which one had hith-
erto been unmindful. Needless to say the act of interpretation in this context was impressive, and the response of the audience was equally so.[20]

It was after this brilliant presentation that Mathews
asked Wieman to join the faculty, which he did the following year.

As Larry Axel reports, Wieman was to provide a coun-
terpoint and a new focus for the school.

The work of many of the Chicagoans with its focus
on the sociohistorical elements which shaped religious
doctrines often found its controlling imagery in equa-
tions from which God-language was increasingly
absented. Emphasis was placed on social ideals and
the power of those ideals to affect human behavior,
without dependence on the "ontological" grounding of those ideals. The "ultimate" nature of the universe was of little concern, or at least was an area of
inquiry to which the sociohistorical theologians had
little access. By contrast, Wieman came to Chicago
having read Whitehead's works in epistemology and
the philosophy of science, steeped in the emergence
philosophies of the "new physics," prepared to em-
bark upon a theology of "reality" rather than a theology of "human ideals."[21]

Wieman steadfastly pursued his empirical theology with
concern for describing the "sensuous" reality of God.[22] God

was an object of human experience that could be studied and described. Wieman was antagonistic toward any merely conceptual theism and adamant in his method of scientific inquiry toward God. With regard to Whitehead, he was soon to part company and renounce Whitehead's speculative metaphysics. Ironically, the Chicago school came more and more under Whiteheadian influence while Wieman himself, who introduced Whitehead so brilliantly, continued to advocate a stricter empiricism and a more modest metaphysics.

With his emphasis on the sovereignty of God and empirical method, Wieman did nonetheless exert great influence through his teaching and writing. It was thus that Morrison and others could make their claim that with Wieman they had an antidote to Barth.

The Later Years

Upon retirement from the University of Chicago Divinity School in 1947, Wieman soon resumed teaching as a Visiting Professor: three years at the University of Oregon (1948-1951); two years at the University of Houston (1951-1953); a year at Grinnell College (1955-1956), and then ten years at Southern Illinois University (1956-1966). Previous summer teaching had included Union Theological Seminary (1933), University of West Virginia (1945), and then after Chicago at the University of California at Los Angeles (1950), Washington University (1951-1954), Iliff Theological Seminary (1955), and Starr King School for the Ministry (1960).[23]

He continued his writing as well as teaching, and one of his most important books, *Man's Ultimate Commitment*, was published in 1958, followed by *Intellectual Foundation of Faith* in 1961 and *Religious Inquiry* in 1968.

Wieman's "Religious Identity"

As noted above, Wieman distinguished between religion and the institutional church. Although he had been ordained a Presbyterian minister, he was antagonistic to Christianity during much of the 1930s. He wished to describe and understand God in empirical terms understandable to all persons. To strengthen only the faith of Christian believers was not his purpose.

For a brief period, however, he gave more explicit attention to Christian language and for the *Christian Century* wrote an article, "Some Blind Spots Removed," for its series, "How My Mind Has Changed." In part he was forced into a strategic counterattack by the prominence of neo-orthodoxy. And in 1946 in *The Source of Human Good*, he employs much more traditional theological language, particularly about Christ and those who followed Jesus, much to the satisfaction of some liberal Christians and to the dismay of more conservative Christians.

Raised and ordained as a Presbyterian, Wieman later became a Unitarian. While in Oregon, he applied for and received ministerial fellowship with the American Unitarian Association. Beacon Press, owned by the Unitarians, published two of his books: *The Directive in History* in 1949 and *Religious Inquiry* in 1968. His articles also appeared in denominational magazines as well as the popular press and scholarly journals. In the 1950s and 1960s he was active with the Unitarian Fellowship in Carbondale, Illinois, and was a speaker for the Laymen's League in the 1960s. Belatedly, in 1975 the Unitarian Universalist Association recognized his contributions and awarded him posthumously, six days after his death, the Award for Distinguished Service to the Cause of Liberal Religion. Henry Nelson Wieman died at the age of ninety on June 19, 1975.

◆ ◆ ◆

"It does not take great numbers to transform a society. Great numbers have never done the work of constructive transformation. Small groups can do it. The greatest evil will always be done by small groups, and also the greatest good."[24]

CHAPTER TWO

Wieman as Philosopher of Religion

"Better Socrates unhappy than a pig happy."

Henry Nelson Wieman saw distinct differences between the work of a philosopher of religion and the work of a theologian. Although an ordained minister with a love of worship and theological acuity, it was in the philosophical arena that he chose to concentrate his efforts.

To understand his distinction between the work of the philosopher of religion and the work of the theologian, we first must look at what he meant by religion. Wieman defined it as: "the most comprehensive, overall, ruling commitment, accepted on the belief that this commitment will direct human striving in such a way that human existence will be saved from its self-destructive and degenerative propensities and transformed to contain the fullest content of value that human life can ever embody."[1]

Religion, then, is a ruling commitment that saves us and fulfills us. In applying to Park College, Wieman answered the question, "What is your object in seeking an education?" with one word: power.[2] Similarly, religion is intimately connected with power. For Wieman, an active religious faith, not education alone, gives us power in our lives.

Wieman believed that the most important problem in religious inquiry is to discern what in truth, not simply in belief, operates to transform and to save humankind.[3] It is precisely here at this point that philosophy of religion has a decisive role to play.

Philosophy of religion is an "instrument of detection and discrimination of truth" in the field of religion.[4] It is a branch of philosophy, he argued, that

- inquires into the origin, function, and nature of religion,
- examines the source and validity of the claims that religion makes,
- clarifies the fundamental religious concepts, and
- criticizes the fundamental practices on the basis of a comprehensive survey of religious data.[5]

Within this broad field, Wieman concentrated on two of these four areas: clarifying fundamental concepts and examining the claims of the Christian tradition.

Theology, for Wieman, goes further than philosophy of religion. Theology is a constructive enterprise aimed at enhancing religious life. It is the systematic formulation of religious beliefs with the goal of guiding the conduct of religious living.[6] He suggests that its task is at least two-fold. Not only does theology aim to clarify doctrinal concepts, but it also seeks to nourish and explicate religious symbols, myths, and rituals in order to enrich the life of worship and the conduct of behavior.[7]

What is the difference then between philosophy of religion and theology? To quote Randolph Crump Miller, "At one point, ... [Wieman] suggested that the philosopher of religion is like the dietitian who knows what reality consists of, while the theologian is like the cook who provides a tasty meal."[8]

Wieman was by no means modest in his goals. He believed that as a philosopher of religion he had the special task of saving theology.[9] In *The Growth of Religion* in 1938, he states his conviction that theology had lost its grip on religious reality and that the forms of expression which it employed "have become unusable by the modern mind."[10] Specifically, he spoke out against dualistic supernaturalism.

Philosophy of religion is the bedrock of theology in its analytic task. Because of the failure of theology, philosophy of religion must step in with "the cold tools of intellectual inquiry without regard for the symbols and patterns that express the ardor of religious devotion."[11] Because of the failure of theology, philosophy of religion must now specify "correctly the distinguishing structure of the divine presence which saves and transforms when men and women give themselves to its sovereign control."[12]

With this self-understanding, Wieman saw his task as that of providing descriptively true statements about God and about God's working in the world. He realized that philosophy of religion could provide only a minimal definition because intellectual concepts are relatively barren of the rich, qualitative meaning that theological symbols convey. Nonetheless, he believed that his was a fundamentally important job. He worked under the assumption that with a "clarified concept. . . we know that the reality in question is an indubitable part of our experienced world."[13] Thus, Wieman intended to provide clarified concepts that would be of use to theology and understandable to the "modern mind."

This task of rescuing theology remained equally clear in his later writings. In 1961 Wieman stated, "Religious language as it prevails today is a tangle of ambiguities, illusions, diverse and unanalyzed meanings."[14] He again emphasized the need for language that is "correctly descriptive" of "what it is to which we give ourselves in religious devotion to be transformed by it as we cannot transform ourselves."[15]

Wieman's concern for clear concepts that will save theology has the practical purpose of saving humankind. Yes, theology is that important.

He believed that it is only through religious devotion to a saving Creativity that humans are able to act responsibly and will be able to survive. The problem of physical survival of humankind on this planet is one of Wieman's recurring concerns. In analyzing the human situation, he finds that humankind and civilization have progressed to a point of global interdependence. Through mass media and modern technology, the world has effectively decreased in size. At the same time, we have also increased our control and power to the point that we are capable of destroying the world and everything on it many times over. Yet, in the face of this power and this new global situation, we have so far failed to find a way to resolve peacefully the differences among peoples.[16]

In Wieman's analysis, there is a cultural malaise that

has been fostered in part by an emphasis on the relativity of all moral values, the relativity of space and of time, and thus the relativity of all existence. Evolutionary theory and anthropological cross-cultural studies, as well as developments in modern physics, have contributed to widespread despair about the existence of any absolutes by which to guide human interactions. The fundamental problem of our age is the lack of a moral code by which women and men can direct their new-found power.[17] It is in this context that Wieman's recurring affirmation of God's sovereignty arises.

Wieman foresees three possibilities for the human future. First, humankind may destroy itself or at least its most developed civilizations. Second, we may fall under the domination of a ruling elite that will ruthlessly set policies for its own benefit with the subjugation of other peoples. Third, national leaders and other powerful individuals may commit themselves to the process of creative interchange whereby we learn to cooperate with each other for mutual benefit.[18]

Thus, Wieman believes that the world is at a point of transition that will lead to humanity's demise, to our humiliation, or to new and greater possibilities. This theme reappears throughout his books from *Now We Must Choose* (1941) to *Religious Inquiry* (1968). Although he discusses the need for basic institutional reforms of government, industry, education, and the church, his solution focuses on the role of persons who commit themselves to the ruling, transforming creativity that operates in human life.[19]

This brings the discussion back to a focus on individual religious commitment, which will be taken up under his doctrine of salvation. The section on Wieman's doctrine of humanity will present his analysis of the human condition, the problems that we must overcome, and the sources of hope.

In brief, Wieman saw his role as that of a philosopher of religion who could provide desperately needed clarity to theological concepts and who could provide an adequate temporal universal by means of the concept of a structure of creativity. These clarified concepts could then be used in guiding human commitment toward cooperation in God's working in the world and in living religiously.

Theological Cornerstones

Before a discussion of Wieman's method is begun, several theological concerns that colored his thought should be presented. The first, already noted, is his soteriological focus with its emphasis on improving the quality of human living on earth. For Wieman, the "religious problem is rightly called the problem of human salvation."[20]

In connection with this, Wieman expresses a profound concern for devotion to the creative process (God) rather than to created goods.[21] His is a call to be faithful to the First Commandment. Idolatry is insidious and pervasive, but commitment to God as Creativity is what can lead to our greatest fulfillment.

The sovereignty of God that initiates and acts in history is the most important aspect and continuing focus of Wieman's thought. God is an inescapable fact of existence for Wieman.[22] God's existence is not a question that is worth very much discussion, nor is Wieman in his writings seeking to provide a proof for the existence of God. Rather he is trying to provide a clear, minimal descriptive definition of God who acts in life and human affairs. He is seeking to provide a concept that, when employed, will aid the individual in recognizing the reality that has existed all along. In all of this there is a latent Calvinism. It appears also in Wieman's grounding of the knowledge of God and humankind in actual concrete events of human living. That is, one can only speak meaningfully about either God or humanity in relationship to the other. Unlike Calvin's thought however, we humans also retain freedom and dignity as agents who can meet required conditions. Human co-creativity with the divine is affirmed.

Philosophical Method

Having identified his goals (a philosopher of religion intent on offering clarified concepts of God and thereby saving theology) and his theological concerns (God's sovereignty and human freedom, co-creativity, and idolatry), we turn to Wieman's philosophical method and presuppositions.

Pragmatism

Wieman embraced the pragmatism of William James and John Dewey.[23] Already apparent is Wieman's instrumentalism in his concern for clear concepts. As a pragmatist, Wieman believed that knowledge should be wondered over and that it is not final.[24] He employed what he usually refered to as a scientific method of hypothesizing, selecting data for observation, finding agreement among observers, and then testing his conclusions for logical coherence. In this way, knowledge becomes self-correcting although it is clearly tentative.[25]

Empiricism

Wieman, as Randolph Crump Miller has observed, upholds the American spirit in theology, which is characterized by empiricism, pragmatism, and a metaphysics that reflects both pluralism and process.[26] J. A. Martin adds that Wieman's empiricism has been the most consistent and thoroughgoing of any American philosopher of religion or theologian.[27]

There are different empiricisms, but each begins with sense experience as the primary source of human knowledge. Wieman states, "We can have no spiritual experience which does not include sense experience, because the living organism is always sensing.... Every power of cognition, every power of appreciation, devotion, love and aspiration requires sense experience in its beginning and in its development."[28]

Thus, God too is an object of experience and to be known as we know any other sense data.[29] We take our raw experience and conceptualize, interpret, and systematize it, whereupon we test it against experience and further refine our concepts.

Miller warns in this approach that much "depends on the presuppositions of the original observer, ... [the] criteria for selecting data, and the way in which the data are interpreted."[30] Thus, in exploring his metaphysics it is necessary to look at Wieman's presuppositions and the way he interprets experience.

A Minimal Process Metaphysics

Wieman keeps his process metaphysics at a minimum.[31] He takes from Whitehead the ontological principle that what is real interacts and what is not real does not. But, he refuses to speculate metaphysically the way Whitehead does (e.g., about the consequent nature of God); such rationalist speculation violates his more rigorous empiricism.

Early in his career he did engage in cosmological speculation. In *Methods of Private Religious Living*, he writes almost lyrically, "God is the integrating process at work in the universe.... This process of progressive integration which we see at work in human society is cosmic in its scope. Electrons interact in such a way as to make atoms, atoms to make molecules, molecules to make cells, cells to make living organisms, living organisms to make individual minds and human society."[32]

Here he explicitly identifies this idea of God with Whitehead's principle of concretion among others, but he hedges on the question of such a "process controlling the universe as a whole."

The empirical mind at work declares, "We are not saying that the whole universe in every phase of its being is steadily moving toward increased integration. We are only saying that amid all the different tendencies of the universe, this progressive integrating tendency is one."[33]

And is it monistic? Is there just one integrating process?

Maybe, maybe not. But there is at least one!

Wieman, in his later works, affirms a limited metaphysics of creativity, but is no longer willing to speculate in the ways that Whitehead and Hartshorne prefer. Increasingly, Wieman looked at the world of human events and interpersonal communication in his metaphysical concerns.[34]

Nonetheless, a holistic, organic interrelatedness and an evolutionary approach lurk in the background. The naturalism that he espouses reflects these two elements. Wieman does grant that metaphysics may provide a vision of the world that is sometimes useful, but it becomes an evil when it obstructs human commitment to creativity.[35]

Wieman's Naturalism

Wieman identifies his naturalism as a form of contextualism that he calls "creative."[36] Although he upholds a process metaphysics, his contextualism, unlike contextualism properly speaking, holds that change is not ultimate. In Wieman's view, the unifying process of creativity makes for a unity in the midst of flux.[37] His naturalism also avoids the spirit/material dualism of so much of Western philosophy and theology.

Central to Wieman's contextualism is a focus on the felt-quality embedded in the structures of events. Wieman used "creative" contextualism as his "world hypothesis" because he believed that it was the most pragmatic way to provide accurate descriptions of experience that would be useful in guiding human living.[38]

Epistemology

To understand Wieman's realistic epistemology and philosophy of religion, it is necessary to describe several of the basic categories that are key to his thought: felt quality, events, structures, and value.

For Wieman, quality is "the ultimate substance of the world out of which all else is made."[39] This is true because "relative to human experience, all energy is quality, and every event is quality."[40] "Everything that enters consciousness as immediately felt is quality; hence we discover qualities by inspecting the content of immediate awareness."[41] And, "quality is concrete reality, the only concrete reality there is.... Quality is the concrete actual event; it is ontological reality. It is what we find the existing world to be in the last analysis; and beyond the existing world there is nothing save possibilities."[42]

That is to say, Wieman's focus on quality derives from his belief that "every event accessible to human experience is a quality or a complex of qualities."[43] Our immediate sense experience involves the sensing of qualities or impressions of objects. When we see a red barn, we first of all sense the quality of "redness" before cognizing either "red" or "barn."

Events may be looked at in either of two ways. First, one can look for the qualities in order to appreciate the event in its richness. Or one can analyze the strands within the event in order to increase practical control and understanding. The former is appreciative, but not analytic. The latter is informative, although relatively barren of felt quality.[44] Both the appreciative and the analytic are important.

The world and events in the world are infinitely rich with felt quality, but the mind is able to find order only as it discerns structures. A structure is an abstraction, a concept, that the mind formulates in order to organize experience. "'Structure' is the name we give to the demarcations and interrelations of events whereby we can apprehend them as different events and yet in meaningful relation to one another."[45]

The mind, by providing structures to qualitative events helps us organize the world. But, there is also a determinative order of existence that helps create the mind. Thus, "The 'world' that we experience arises from the cooperation of two factors. One is the response of the organism including all the constructive powers of the mind; the other is the play of influence upon the organism from the outside."[46]

This is essentially a structuralist view of the mind inasmuch as we gain knowledge through a process of assimilation and accommodation. To repeat: There are constitutive structures of the mind that actively structure experience. At the same time, there are structures to events that help create the mind. In this sense, the universe is not simply waiting to be discovered. Rather it is created by the creativity operating in human existence.[47]

The creative process that Wieman discerns is the only ultimate constitutive structure because it is present in the process of obtaining all knowledge, and it is present in all cognizing. "The constitutive structure of the universe (creativity) is identical with the constitutive structure of the mind."[48] This means that the "appreciable world and the appreciating mind are one single order of existence."[49]

Value Theory

For Wieman, value theory plays a crucial role in his thinking. In *The Source of Human Good*, Wieman is wrestling with value theory and God's role as creator of human good. Value is found in the increase of qualitative meaning, namely the rich, felt quality of events. More precisely, qualitative meaning is that connection between events whereby the present happening conveys to me the qualities of other happenings and some qualities pertaining to what will happen in the future, as the future is interpreted by the past.[50]

Qualitative meaning is created good and has intrinsic value. In Wieman's metaphysics, "the goal of life (the conservation and increase of value) is to structure the world so that qualities will be more appreciable."[51] The next chapter will examine the Creative Event, which is both the source of human good and the source of increased value and meaning.

In this realistic epistemology, quality and value exist before truth.[52] Truth is "any specifiable structure pertaining to events and their possibilities."[53] It is "an artificial and abstract version of that infinite complexity of structure characterizing actual events and possibilities."[54] Knowledge arises when the specifiable structures are in fact specified.[55]

Wieman's empiricism focuses on all of experience as the experience of rich, felt quality from which structures may be specified and described, yielding truth and knowledge. True concepts are forms of possibility that pertain to actual events in existence and are useful to increase appreciation and to guide action. Wieman's scientific method looks to concrete actual events against which he tests his concepts about that reality which operates in the world and which has the power to transform human living as humans cannot transform themselves.

Wieman's empirical, pragmatic method intends a tentativeness and open-mindedness. Yet he believes that in creative events (the process of creativity) he has found an ultimate constituent of reality. The creative event (or creative interchange) creates all value that is the felt quality that may arise from the interconnections and relations among events.

◆ ◆ ◆

Henry Nelson Wieman perceived his role to be that of a philosopher of religion and empirical theologian. It was his conviction that clear, cogent concepts about God that were empirically grounded could give guidance to life so that we might live most fully and usefully.

His approach was pragmatic, empirical and naturalistic. His realistic epistemology led him to appreciate the felt qualities of experience. Upon analysis of experience, he suggests/declares that a structure of creativity is evident, and it is absolutely trustworthy. Whatever is absolutely trustworthy may also legitimately be designated as God.

Having focused so much on his intellectual approach, I would add words of caution from Wieman about what is truly important.

Religion, in one sense, is like baseball or any other form of play or art. The professionals who play in the big leagues render a great service to baseball. Baseball would certainly not pervade our national life as it does if it were not for these big leagues. But if you want to find out the true spirit of baseball in all the glory of a passion, you must not go to the big leagues. You must go to the backyard, the sandlot, the side street, and the school ground. There it is not a profession, it is a passion. When a passion becomes a profession, it often ceases to be a passion. That is as true of religion as it is of baseball. Among the professionals you find a superb mastery and a great technique, but not too frequently the pure devotion. Perhaps in baseball the passion is not too important, but in religion it is all important. A religion that is not passionate simply is not worth considering. Therefore, I say, we need more sandlot religion. The professional, whether White Sox or Methodist, controls inordinately our baseball and our religion.[56]

The Creative Event (God) was Wieman's passion, and Wieman's theocentrism is the topic of the next chapter. It will also look further at Wieman as an empirical theologian and his status as a Christian theologian.

CHAPTER THREE

Wieman as Theologian

"What makes one feel at home in the universe is one's beliefs about the universe, and the part and place of human life in it. This system of beliefs is the foundation of one's sense of inner security, and is the basis for the organization of oneself and one's characteristic behavior. When these beliefs are disordered or nullified, life loses its order and meaning.... There are ... certain searchers in the field, who while holding their findings to the discipline of rigid test are exploring with relatively open minds the possibilities of meaning and value wherever these seem likely to be found."

With regard to the historical context of Wieman's thought, he embraced the modernist spirit of liberal theology, yet repudiated the anthropocentric, humanistic liberalism of the 1930s. His naturalistic theism alienated fundamentalists, proponents of neo-orthodoxy, and liberal humanists. Nonetheless, Wieman pursued his own course and won adherents to empirical theology, first as a member of the faculty of the University of Chicago Divinity School from 1927 to 1947 and, later, still writing and teaching during a very active "retirement."[1] Charles Clayton Morrison, editor of the *Christian Century*, "spoke for many ... midwestern liberals in his memorable words, 'I don't need Barth! Wieman is my Barth!'"[2]

In addition, as outlined in the previous chapter, Wieman saw his task first and foremost within the realm of philosophy of religion. Wieman was not a systematic theologian; he did not see that as his calling. Indeed, he would be wary of such an enterprise lest the doctrines themselves be given greater precedence than the actual creativity at work in the midst of human living.

And, as we shall see, Wieman was not unequivocally a Christian theologian, although he felt his roots in the Christian tradition and could write with great emotion about the saving significance of the Christ-event. In his later years, Wieman refused to label himself either as a Christian or as a non-Christian, nor did he accept the name of either theist or religious humanist.[3]

The Creative Event and Wieman's Theocentrism

Wieman concerned himself throughout his career with specifying that which operates in human existence which transforms and save humans and increases creative good. For him, the power that does this is synonymous with the term God.

God, for Wieman, is an indubitable fact of existence. As noted, in his "Intellectual Autobiography" he recalls the force and sustaining power of a mystical experience of God.[4]

Although Wieman respects mystical experiences for the richness of quality that they embody, he resolutely denies that they may provide any knowledge. He values these richly felt experiences, but as a philosopher of religion he is concerned with appropriating these experiences intellectually. One might hypothesize psychologically that Wieman's career arose as an effort to make intellectual sense out of his own mystical experience. And as previously noted, Wieman sought to present a clarified concept of God by which to revitalize theology and religion.

In his early writings, Wieman's concern for an operational concept of God that derived from value theory is evident. For example, in *The Issues of Life* he defines God as a structure of existence and possibility that allows for the achievement of the greatest human good.[5] But, it is in *The Source of Human Good* that Wieman describes the creative event as the means by which value increases in the world.

> The creative event increases good because it produces qualitative meaning, which thus leads to increased appreciation and awareness of events and a web of richer meaning. The good produced is absolute because it is good under all circumstances and under all conditions; it is unlimited, infinite in value, unqualified and entirely trustworthy.[6]

Creative events involve four subevents. Succinctly, they are:

- an emerging awareness in the individual of qualitative meaning communicated to oneself from some other organism,

- integrating of new meanings with the old,
- an expanding appreciation of the appreciable world, and
- a widening and deepening community among participants in the creative event.[7]

The creative event as outlined above is grounded empirically in interpersonal interaction. Wieman discussed the creative event most frequently in interpersonal terms. In *Man's Ultimate Commitment* he describes creative intercommunication or interchange as:

- an expansion of the range and diversity of what one can know, evaluate, and control,
- an increasing capacity to appreciate others,
- an increasing personal freedom, and
- an increasing ability to integrate appreciatively one's experience.[8] This is deemed to be good because it allows for a new structure of interrelatedness whereby events are discriminated and related in a manner not before possible.[9]

Later he would speak of five dimensions of transformation: increasing knowledge, expanding awareness and richness of experience, deepening of community with others, growing ability to exercise mutual power and control over happenings, and discernment of the preciousness of persons.[10]

William Minor captures the rhythmic, dynamic element of the creative event and writes about the "deep and intense contrasts: rhythmic contrasts/between emerging imaginative insights/and those already had/in critical creative interaction/occurring within expanding appreciative consciousness/creating novel unity/in one's expanding world/ creating deeper contrasts/with other expanding worlds/undergoing creative critical interchange/conflict creating community."[11]

Wieman also speaks of the process of creativity as the more general process found in concrete creative events. This is what may be called a second order abstraction on Wieman's part. ("Creative event" is the first order, and "process of creativity" is the second order.) Although he employs both types of statements, Wieman's ultimate allegiance is with the concrete events themselves and not with the more abstract term. No matter which term Wieman prefers to use at any given point in his writings, he is describing a continuous process in the world that leads to an increase of value.

It is axiomatic for Wieman that God is the name for the ultimate transforming reality that increases human good. The section dealing with Wieman's doctrine of God will explore further the equating of God with the creative event and the source of human good.

The philosophical position that Wieman defends is taken on the pragmatic grounds that that is the best way for a "modern mind" to understand the notion (and reality) of deity. Immediately, Wieman has limited his potential audience to those who share his own disillusionment with traditional use and interpretation of Christian language and symbols. And it is to be expected that many of those who find Christian language and symbols effective to express their relationship to God and the universe will see Wieman's perspective as insufficient, if not heretical.

Nonetheless, for others Wieman provides a way to revitalize Christianity and enables it to speak to the "modern mind."

John Bennett has concurred in asserting Wieman's importance as one who shaped a generation of intellectually concerned ministers in the Midwest.[12]

For some others, Wieman's language may simply be mystifying or confusing or, for the devoted humanist, irrelevant. Yet, for still others, Wieman's thought offers a foundation for natural and/or contextual theologies and powerfully revitalizes the concept of God, but without necessary recourse to the Christian framework.

A Minimal, Natural Theology

Although Wieman himself claimed to be a philosopher of religion, his work has also been a theological task. Randolph Crump Miller, for example, evaluates Wieman's work primarily in the area of natural theology. He calls Wieman an empirical theologian who, by establishing an immanent deity in minimum terms provides a basis for constructing a full-fledged theology.[13]

Wieman also saw himself as a theologian when "theology means a seeking to understand what calls for humanity's ruling commitment by reason of its creative and saving power."[14] He is also sensitive to his own demand that theology respond to the findings of modern science. But he admits that "theology must still then go further—to interpret and symbolize this creativity in such a way that women and men can find it operating in their own lives, in all their social relations, and throughout human history."[15]

As discussed, Wieman has concentrated on the philosophical task of refining the concept and describing the working of creative events. In concentrating on interpreting "this creativity," he has pursued the theological task of symbolizing creativity only incidentally. He is acutely aware of the importance of myth, symbol, and ritual in the life of worship, and in many of his books he discusses worship, prayer, myth, and symbol. Because he has not devoted his writings to the symbolizing activity, however, he does not develop the kind of "full-fledged" theology of which Miller speaks.[16]

A second element of Wieman's empirical theology that distinguishes itself from others is his avoidance of speculative metaphysics. The neoclassical metaphysics of a Hartshorne, for example, are of no utility to Wieman. Similarly, in *Religious Inquiry* he argues against ontologists like Plotinus or Tillich.

As discussed in the previous chapter, Wieman's metaphysics centers on the process of creativity as evident in human relationships. His devotion is to creative interchange itself. Wieman argues that it is precisely this process and reality of creative interchange arising from reflection and dialogue that produces Hartshorne's vision of the cosmos and Tillich's of Being itself.

As a Christian Theologian

Wieman, as already noted, is an empirical theologian and

philosopher of religion who minimizes analogical inference and who focused on the ruling sovereignty of God as present in creative events. Furthermore, he has engaged in a program of "rigorous de-mythologization" of Christian doctrine by means of the metaphysical and axiological framework outlined above.[17] Many have deemed him to be a Christian theologian while others have called him a heretic. He believes firmly that one cannot be religious in general and that one must take seriously one's own religious heritage.[18] He himself speaks fondly of his Christian background.[19] But, he is also evasive when it comes to being labeled a Christian. Ultimately, Wieman is disparaging of labels and beckons us back to the felt quality of experience, its richness, beauty, and transforming power in Creative Events.

Although taking issue with Wieman on many specific points, both Randolph Crump Miller and Daniel Day Williams place Wieman within the Christian theological tradition.[20] Williams especially emphasizes this in his article, "Wieman as a Christian Theologian." His thesis is that "Wieman's thought arises within the Christian community as an expression of the essential truth of the Christian faith."[21] Bernard Loomer adds that the "questions he asks and the answers he gives are undeniably Christian."[22]

Walter M. Horton correctly notes that "Wieman's theology makes its nearest approach to the historic faith of the Christian Church" in his christological statements.[23] Wieman shows his Christian background and respect for Christian symbols when he states:

This creativity must be interpreted in such a way that the churches can make it the central theme of all their services, either directly or indirectly, just as many churches now make "Christ" their central theme. Indeed, when "Christ" is identified with the way of life revealed in the fellowship of Jesus, we find therein that creativity which expands the activities of mutual support across conflicts and diversities. How people can best be led to understand this creativity is by identifying it with the revelation in Christ; that can be done in full honesty and complete accord with known facts, provided this revelation is freed from supernaturalism, from what transcends the universe and from identification with the universe.[24]

Wieman's christological statements will be examined in greater detail in a later section.

Other theologians such as Georges Florovsky refuse to label Wieman's thought as Christian. "Wieman readily retains certain bits of Christian phraseology but he uses traditional terms in his own unusual and therefore misleading manner. He admits the impact of Christianity but refuses to admit its uniqueness."[25] Or, as Gustave Weigel has said more pointedly, one

can ask that he refuse the label of Christian theologian. The word "Christian" is an accepted indicator for a well-defined historical tradition. The heart of this tradition is the affirmation of the transcendence of God and divinity of Jesus Christ. To this formal tradition Wieman does not belong. Some Christian characteristics are his, but not the essential core. I would gently suggest that Wieman call himself a post-Christian. Some word like that would adequately describe his position.[26]

In his response to Weigel, Wieman states, "I have no zeal to appropriate to myself the name of Christian if anyone wishes to dispute my right to this classification."[27] But he goes on to argue for a contemporary Christian language rather than an archaic one. He also points out that Christianity has taken diverse forms and elsewhere notes that Christianity has developed such diversity that "the answer given to the religious question in one form often contradicts the answer given in other forms. . . . (T)he meaning of the words "revelation of God in Christ" is one of the most controversial questions in the Christian faith."[28]

Usually, Wieman is evasive about his self-understanding as a Christian and as a Christian theologian despite his fond memories of his Christian upbringing. For example, Wieman, when asked directly if his intent is to be a Christian theologian, answers:

> I find it difficult to answer this question without causing misunderstanding. Certainly I am shaped and biased by the tradition in which I was reared. The Christian tradition with its error, its evil and its truth, is my chief resource. Yet I strongly resent the current practice of appealing to the Christian and Jewish tradition as being the guide of life and identifying this

tradition with God rather than seeking what operates in all human life to create, save and transform....
I suppose that nearly every one is a mixture of currents and cannot be placed neatly in any one of them.[29]

In the same volume, he responds to Walter Horton: "Let me state that I do not think of Jesus as the highest product of the Creative Process. The revelation of God in Christ should never be identified with the man Jesus. The revelation of God is the transforming power which operated in the fellowship of Jesus and continues to operate today when required conditions are present."[30]

This is exactly the kind of rigorous demythologization of which Williams speaks and to which Florovsky and Weigel object.

Finally, we may see Wieman's understanding of what it means to be a Christian in one of his earliest books, *The Issues of Life*. He describes a Christian as one who has access to certain clues, insights, and suggestions in her or his search for the greatest good. Although the same data of historic conditions, of biblical witness, and of worship are open to all observers, the Christian is one who not only studies the tradition, but also "has gotten sufficiently in rapport with the whole movement to discover its significance from the inside."[31] In this sense, Wieman is a Christian, although this may not be acceptable to critics like the Eastern Orthodox Florovsky and Roman Catholic Weigel.[32]

It is clear that Wieman saw his work as being within the Christian tradition and as truly capturing the essence of

Christianity in contemporary, empirical, literal language. The problem is that the "essence" of Christianity is a confusing term and at times useless. Wieman enjoyed pitting theological interpretations such as Barth's and Tillich's against each other.[33] Wieman's allegiance to Christianity indicates that this was the religious tradition of which he was a part and that for him best symbolized the concrete reality of creativity that has the power to transform and to save humankind.

What Wieman refuses to do is to judge the truth of a statement solely by its presence within the Bible or within the Christian tradition. This leads us to Wieman's concepts of authority and revelation.

Wieman's Concepts of Authority and Revelation

As noted in the previous chapter, truth and knowledge in Wieman's system pertain to the description and specification of structures that reflect actual experience. The "scientific method" that Wieman employs to study empirical events and to gain knowledge is the authority to which Wieman appeals. In his view, authority derives either from dogma or from a reliable method for detecting error and gathering evidence.[34]

"Knowledge" based on dogmatic claims usually derives from traditions, intuitions, or revelation. For Wieman, however, such claims having nothing to do with knowledge or truth. Wieman rejects statements of truth that are advanced simply by virtue of their being a part of the biblical story or Christian tradition.[35]

Wieman calls for evidence for belief, and at the height of the Fundamentalist controversy in the 1920s, characterized by declarations of the literal inerrancy of the Bible, he published an article in *The New Republic* titled "Religion in Dreamland." The religion of dreamland seems easy and lovely at first. But it leads ultimately to intolerance and the grossest superstitions, to the use of legislation, persecution, and war to enforce its convictions. When one discards the persuasiveness of evidence and fairness in reasoning together, there is no way to defend and propagate the faith save emotional contagion and violence.[36]

To be sure, Wieman values intuition because it is identical with the second subevent of the creative event; intuition is the integration of a new event with the old.[37] However, intuition, like tradition, must be tested against experience for reasonable coherence. Only then will Wieman accept these kinds of hypotheses as reflecting truth or leading to knowledge.[38]

Similarly, revelation is important. "Revelation is some historic event that changes life so radically that realities previously beyond the reach of discovery become apparent to those whose lives are thus changed."[39] Wieman discusses the raising of the creative event to dominance in the lives of Jesus' disciples as such a revelation.[40] With this revelation came transformation, faith, and salvation in the fellowship of the disciples. In this way, revelation is identified with God's acts of self-disclosure.[41] But revelation by itself does not yield truth or knowledge. Knowledge, which is a critical, analytical, intellectual process, may have followed afterward, but cannot be identified with revelation itself.

For Wieman, the tests of truth must come from his method of observation, agreement between observers, and logical coherence. He proceeds in this way to test the implications and conclusions of tradition, intuitions, and revelation. "Nothing but persistent and rigorous inquiry and the evidence thus found can support any teaching."[42]

Finally, he holds that this method must be used with competence. That is, one must be thoroughly trained through "rigorous discipline" in order to achieve the competence required in the intellectual work of religious inquiry.[43]

Thus, Wieman believes that traditional or biblical dogma, intuition, and revelation are valuable, but that they must be held in tension with new evidence and further testing. As the title of his final book indicates, Wieman's concern is for continuing *Religious Inquiry*.

Ultimately, the truths and teachings that one discovers to have experiential testability, validity, and coherence, as well as instrumental value, will remain tentative rather than absolute and final. Although at times appearing to hold his own concepts of creativity and the creative event dogmatically, Wieman feels that this concept meets the tests that he has set forth. But he admits that he no doubt is partially in error regarding the description of the creative event that he has advanced.

I know that I cannot be in error in holding the belief that I am at least partially in error concerning the character of the reality to which I am ultimately committed. Hence I know with certainty that I am ulti-

mately given to what is more than, and in some respects different from, everything affirmed in this book
[*Man's Ultimate Commitment*]. With this triumph
over error I make my last commitment: I cast my
error, my failure, and my guilt into the keeping of
creative and transforming power.[44]

Thus, he affirms that the work of conceptual clarification must always continue.

Nevertheless, it is important to remember again that
transforming experiences (with increase of value and quality) take precedence over statements of truth and knowledge in Wieman's perspective. Knowledge and truth should
be servants of faith and of the increase of value, the good.
Knowledge and truth are to direct the life of worship and
day by day action in the service of creative good.[45]

The following two chapters will clarify the theological
doctrines that are implicit in Wieman's books, but that he
himself did not systematize. This systematic approach to
Wieman's thought is an effort to elucidate his philosophy
and to clarify his relationship to the still relevant questions
with which Christian theologians have traditionally concerned themselves.

CHAPTER FOUR

Wieman's Theological Doctrines

"Doctrines take on importance only as pointers to direct attention and commitment to the new order of events, namely, creative good dominant over created good in the devotion of women and men."

In his writings Henry Nelson Wieman engages in both philosophy of religion and philosophical theology. At points, he even proclaims an almost ecstatic confessional theology. Because of this shifting of attitude and tone, a systematic theological treatment of his thought becomes useful.

To systematize Wieman's philosophy is a matter of clarifying his relationship to the questions and answers with which Christian theologians have traditionally concerned themselves. This exercise also recognizes that these traditional doctrines of faith—the systematic theologian's categories—reflect deep-seated human curiosity, yearning, fear, and hope. These doctrines are the result of wrestling with basic questions about:

- authority (How do we know what to believe?)
- God and the cosmos (Is anything trustworthy? Is the

Universe friendly or hostile, ordered or chaotic?)
- human nature (Who and what are we?)
- good and evil (How do we know the good and why is there evil?)
- salvation (How do we become saved?)
- Jesus (Who was he and what difference does it make?)
- history and the future, that is, eschatology (Is there meaning in history and what happens ultimately?)
- community (Traditionally speaking, what is the role of the church?).

Because of the fundamental nature of these questions and to help locate Wieman's distinctive contribution in the larger community of theologians, this chapter will address them, except for the matter of authority. The previous chapter considered this question about how we decide what it is that we should believe (reason, intuition, revelation, and/or experience). Wieman's work arises within a Christian context, but as we shall see, it takes its own distinctive direction.

In this undertaking I am mindful of Wieman's comment that "the tragedy of humanity and our generic sin is to try to put all existence into servitude of specifiable structures of truth."[1] These "truths" that we may discern are, in fact, but a very "thin layer of oil" over the ocean of the "infinitely complex structure" of our world.[2] He confesses that his own preoccupation with specifiable structures (with truth-seeking) "is a mere accident of his scholarly objectives."[3]

God

As already noted, Wieman seeks a minimal definition of God that will aid the process of revitalizing theology in the twentieth century. And he identifies God's working in the world with creative events. The fourfold creative event, as discussed above, becomes the key to an understanding of Wieman's philosophy of religion and of his implicit theological position.

This fourfold event includes (1) greater awareness and sensitivity with emergent perspectives, (2) progressive integrations, (3) expanded appreciations, and (4) growth of community.

Also as noted above, Wieman does not set out to prove the existence of God. Humans "first experience God not knowing it is God, and then later get the criteria to recognize deity in what has been with them all the time."[4] Furthermore, God, which he had hypothesized earlier as the "growth of connections between activities which are appreciable,"[5] and later as the creative event, is much more than we can comprehend.[6] Wieman is fully aware that conceptual, descriptive definitions in no way capture the totality that is God. Regarding these definitions, he states: "look upon your idea of God as a very poor, very unsatisfactory, extremely inadequate instrument, to be used only because you have nothing better for the time being, to be discarded just as soon as you can find a better."[7] Thus, any concept of God is operational, experimental, and directive.[8]

God in History and as the Source of Value

The fourfold creative event, which Wieman concludes to be an accurate description of God's working, is a process description of two aspects of God's reality: God's temporal activity and God as the source of human value—the good.

First, Wieman is concerned to go behind the Greek philosophical notion of God as the Ideal and to recapture the Hebraic concept of God who acts in history, hence the emphasis on actual events.[9] Second, he believes that God's activity can best be approached through an axiological, rather than an ontological, framework. God, no matter how God is conceived, is that which creates value in the world. The creative event that creates value in human life is naturally to be connected with the traditional term "God."[10]

Wieman admits that equating the creative event with God might lead to confusion. But he argues pragmatically that humans need some way to designate their primary commitment and to practice that commitment.[11] And God is the term that has been used to convey human ultimate commitment.

Furthermore, he asserts that the term "God" is as necessary for worship as the term "creative event" is for philosophical discourse. Once again, we must remember that, for Wieman, God is an experienced reality and not simply an idea that helps to make the world more intelligible. Nor is God simply a moral construct to guide conduct. God is not reducible to a matter of moral pragmatism for human betterment.[12]

Development of Wieman's Concept of God

Wieman's concept of God (the concretized universal that he describes as creativity) reflects the influence of many thinkers, including Bergson, Royce, Hocking, Perry, and then for a brief time, Whitehead. In *The Wrestle of Religion with Truth* (1927), God is the principle of concretion, just as Whitehead formulated it.[13] (However, as already noted he comes to reject Whitehead's further speculation about the primordial and consequent natures of God.)[14]

By 1930 in *The Issues of Life*, God is defined as a structure of existence and possibility that allows for the possibility and the achievability of the greatest good through human effort.[15] God, as structure of existence and possibility, is already implied in the notion of a principle of concretion. The interrelatedness of all that is and the dependence of anything on the structure of every other thing suggests an order of existence in which the possibilities are determined and ordered.

The rational analysis of structures, possibilities, and the Ideal gives an ontological focus to Wieman's thought at this stage and displays an interest in a rational, process metaphysics less empirical than his later work.

To continue a moment longer: His thesis is that God is necessarily involved in the attainment of the Ideal—the greatest good possible through human effort. The Ideal is possibility to be achieved; God is "that order of existence and possibility by virtue of which the greatest possible good is truly a possibility and can be achieved by human effort."[16] Without God, the Ideal would remain an abstract possibility without any chance of being actualized. Thus, only through God can the Ideal be achieved; it is necessary in order to achieve the Ideal to deal with the order that makes the Ideal possible, that is, with God. Wieman's early work is replete with this kind of ontological focus with its discussions of an order of existence and possibility. Fortunately, Wieman did not stop here.

From Ontology to the Interpersonal

In this earlier period, he does state, although without great elaboration, that the nature of the order that is God is also the order of love and the order of communication. This is the order of greatest value that leads beyond cooperation into community, communal vision, and the united good.

The concern for the order of love and communication became dominant in *The Source of Human Good*. With the elucidation of the fourfold creative event, Wieman felt that he had in significant measure succeeded in his philosophical task. He had found a way to describe the workings of God that would aid the individual in making a total commitment to God. He had found the clarified concept that might lead the individual to the right attitude by which one could then come to experience God in God's greater fullness—the fullness of the concrete events of everyday life and of worship.

To the question "Where do we find God?" he responds, "In the creative events!" This is the intellectual and philosophical understanding that Wieman offers.

God reaches consciousness on the emotive level through practices of worship and prayer. In religious practices we develop the responsiveness, the appreciative awareness, the pattern of apprehension, and the disposition of commitment of the total personality to God.[17] God's profundity, depth, and character cannot be fully described by a term such as creative event. But God can be experienced more fully in worship than in concepts.

Wieman has accurately been called a Unitarian of the Third Person—the Spirit. Occasionally, Wieman invoked such language, and had he developed a full-fledged theology with attention to the language of worship, he may well have emphasized it. Once again, the essential point is that God is found in human experience on a continuing basis. God may be described in terms of normal, everyday experience in creative events and creative interchange. It is a matter of making ourselves qualified observers and of sensitizing ourselves to God's working—to the presence of the Spirit.[18]

God's "Nature"

We are now ready to examine the kinds of statements that Wieman, as an empiricist, is willing to make about God in response to the question, "What is God's nature?" To be sure, Wieman, by addressing the question, would not wish to imply that God is Being with some essential nature. Wieman nonetheless is willing to compare his concept of creative event, or creative interchange, to categories and attributes that Christian theology has used in order to discuss God's nature.

For Wieman, God is unitary in that the creativity at work in the world is one process.[19] (Note that this is not a strictly empirical conclusion, and recall in earlier work that he was hesitant to affirm this. Nonetheless, Wieman would argue now that it is pragmatically acceptable and can be held experimentally. Having earlier spoken in more cosmic terms, he in later work restrained himself for the sake of an empirical approach.)

- God is suprapersonal, but not supernatural, nor a person or personality.[20]
- God transcends humankind but does not transcend nature or history.[21]
- God is the source of human good and the growth of human value, but is not omnipotent.[22]
- God is creator but requires human cooperation to further human good.[23]
- God participates in the natural order, but Wieman is not a pantheist.[24]
- Wieman has gone so far as to identify God with the symbol "the Father" (although not often), and God assuredly "answers" prayers.[25]
- But, he also speaks about God as the "mothering matrix of existence."[26]
- God also acts as a sovereign judge upon our actions and at times opposes humanity.[27]
- God acts in history and paradigmatically so in the Christ event.[28]
- Finally, God is love and creates community.[29]

Thus, God as the creative event or creativity takes on familiar attributes of the Christian tradition. God is creator, the source of our salvation, judge and ruler of history, self-revealing in Christ, and the initiator of human community arising in the fellowship of Jesus.[30]

But, God is not a person, a mind, an omnipotent being, or a transcendent being beyond nature and history. Nevertheless, Wieman concedes that God may be thought of as a person for purposes of worship. He understands the intense human need to establish personal relationships. However, he finds this habit to be so dangerous (in terms of leaving false ideas of God) that it should be avoided.[31]

God is involved in the creation of personality and mind, but is not to be equated with mind, which is solely a human attribute.

God is not all powerful in Wieman's view because value is lost and irrecoverable in our world.[32] Those who think otherwise, he asserts, do not take the existence of evil in the world with sufficient seriousness.

Finally, the empirical reality of God of which Wieman is aware is always found in events; God beyond either nature or history is a fuzzy abstraction that creates confusion and that has no empirical basis and utility for Wieman.

The existence of a God who answers prayers, yet who is not a person, is on the face of it a confusing question. Wieman handles it through a discussion of prayer as a creative event, that is, an opportunity for personal growth/ transformation, new insight, sensitivity, self-integration, and deepened community.[33] In this way, Wieman finds his concept of God fully applicable to the total worship experience. Indeed, for him it is the precondition for an intelligent commitment to God, to that creative power that actually operates in human existence to transform humans and to save humankind.

Bernard Loomer has beautifully summarized Wieman's approach to God. He states: "Wieman has looked to the experienceable world to discover, if possible, an empirically given, objective, concrete reality upon which all men (and women) are ultimately dependent for their fulfillment, a reality directly experienceable, and known as all other concrete realities are known, a reality efficaciously at work in our midst to redeem us, a reality forever beyond our control, a reality known with such certainty that its existence is beyond debate or doubt, a reality of such value that it is worthy of our deepest trust and loyalty under all circumstances and times and places, a reality of such inexhaustible and transcending goodness that we kneel in awe and reverence, and in relation to whose holiness we recognize our sinful ways. The term 'God' is to be attributed to whatever experienceable and empirical reality meets these criteria."[34] This reality is creativity, and it is truly God. It is to this reality and not to the concept alone that one should commit oneself.

Thus, Wieman's concept of God reflects some of the traditional attributes of God in Christian theology. Yet, it radically departs in other respects. In addition to rejecting ideas of God as person or mind, or omnipotent being or superhistorical being, there remains the question of the centrality of the life and work of Jesus of Nazareth in Wieman's theological understanding. But, before this discussion, we shall consider the elements of Wieman's Doctrine of Humanity and Salvation.

Humanity

"We are made for creative transformation as a bird is made for flight."[35]

Foremost in and throughout Wieman's thought is his theocentrism. Yet, as he spelled out his concept of God as creative event in *The Source of Human Good* and afterwards, the focus is also clearly upon the realm of human interaction. He moved away from the cosmological and ontological speculations to earthly human interaction and particularly to creative intercommunication. It is this focus on human existence that he reiterates in his book *Religious Inquiry* and that leads him to call himself an existentialist (although not to be identified with the philosophical movement of existentialism).[36]

Furthermore, Wieman signed the Humanist Manifesto II, thereby partially identifying himself near his life's end as a humanist. However, he did so only "with qualified support based on its footnote saying that signers may not agree with parts of ... [the statement]."[37] What his signing does show is his continued concern and focus on the human individual and on human responsibility to cooperate in the creative events that increase value.

Blessings

When Wieman turns to humankind to seek its distinguishing characteristics, he discovers several activities or blessings. Primary is our ability to construct imaginative symbols by which we are able to communicate and better appreciate the world. This ability is our greatest gift.[38] He is stating the same thing in another way when he writes: "Human existence is distinguished from every other kind of existence by a creativity that drives toward the indefinite expansion of the range of what can be known, controlled, and valued as good and evil."[39]

This creativity means that humans are valuing creatures at our core.[40] For Wieman, our goal as humans is to survive with the increase of value.[41] Moreover, we humans are the spearhead of creative power that transforms both us and the world.[42] In connection with this creative capacity, humans are also explorers, dreamers, and symbol makers who are not satisfied with existence in which we find ourselves. Women and men are made for this world as long as we are trying to reconstruct it.[43] To be most fully human is to be creative. This is the goal to which human life should be directed, for there is no Godly destiny apart from this.

Wieman also distinguishes humanity from nature and other creatures. A human is the creature who laughs, talks, and plays imaginatively. He or she also uses tools, reasons, worships, and rears a culture.[44] The civilization that arises out of culture is traced back to the unique creative, imagining ability.

Our Greatest Need
At one point, Wieman writes, "Our greatest need is to love and to be loved."[45] There are other needs, to be sure, such as freedom, hope, and physical needs, but the greatest of these is love. The greatest satisfaction of this primary need comes through a commitment to creative interchange, the Creative Event, Creativity. Such a commitment and prac-

tice enable a form of mutuality to arise that is redemptive and transforming, that is godly.

Limitations

Although we humans are creating, valuing creatures, we are also limited in serious respects. In *The Source of Human Good*, Wieman outlined three factors:

First, there are limits to our appreciative capacities. We simply miss a vast amount of the appreciable world in its richness.

Second, self-concern often predominates and perverts the individual, thus leading to distortions of the original self.

Third, there are resistances to change usually because of the narrowness of one's structure of awareness.[46] To these, he adds a discussion of "inertias—insensitivity and resistance to creativity" that may drag us down. Among these are inertias of "inane comfort and ease; of frivolity; of arrogance and complacency; of superficial communication . . . , or the inertia of continuous change, blocking or canceling out every creative transformation; the inertia that issues from a kind of tolerance that hands over to private preference the ultimate decisions concerning matters of supreme importance; the inertia of the cultural crisis that comes when growing insight discerns the relative futility of every high human purpose."[47]

In *Man's Ultimate Commitment*, he elaborates on the numerous means of miscommunication that exist. Rather than being creative, communication can be manipulative, deceptive, reiterative, "other-directed" (to use David Riesman's term), and simply muddled.

These interrelated factors function to limit the individual's ability to act freely and creatively. For Wieman, they are profoundly serious problems for human fulfillment and hinder the original self.

The original self, a term Wieman uses in *Man's Ultimate Commitment*, is full of positive potentials and includes "every experience which the individual can have when we do not conceal and overlay our being with the drab qualities of conventional experience."[48] The original self may be recovered when we reduce to a minimum the "security operations" (a term borrowed from Harry Stack Sullivan's *The Interpersonal Theory of Psychiatry*) that all persons use to protect their egos from imaginary and actual threats.[49] The masks, shields, barriers, and the like that we use define our conventional self. Our original self may wither in the process. "One who no longer feels fear, awe or wonder, can no longer grow."[50]

Original Sin

Wieman firmly believes that because humans inevitably encounter and create limits we must learn to live with and accept our brokenness.[51] He even speaks of Original Sin in the sense that parents transmit to their children their own resistances, fears, and inadequacies plus their frequent concern for created goods rather than creative good.[52]

There are "dark realities" to life that humans must learn to accept. Although Wieman discusses painful realities in terms of (1) those that are built into the nature of things and (2) those that are particularly human, his focus is on humanity's ability to respond creatively in either case. Even death, which Wieman represents as the central painful reality built into nature, should be accepted and understood as actually enabling the creative process to continue.[53]

The sinful nature of humanity is a tendency to turn against the Creator (the creative event—God) and to turn toward the created good. It is human rebellion against God. Wieman defines sin as "any resistance to creativity for which a person is responsible."[54] And, often, it is corporate and social, as well as personal.

Evil

Evil, then, is any act that thwarts creativity. The structure of the world, society, and human nature is such that creativity may be unfulfilled, lost, denied, or resisted. But, as far as Wieman can discern and conclude, evil is not an external, active agent, being, or power.

The evil, which we are heir to, manifests itself in several ways. First, there is inner conflict which can dominate, as in the classic expression: "What I would not, that I do."

Second, evil appears as triviality, futility, and unendurable boredom, which may appear when one awakens to the "contrast between one's original experience with its potentialities and its freedom over against the mechanisms of adjustment demanded by an impersonal social order."[55]

Third, there is the sense of guilt that arises from refusing to choose vibrant living in favor of drifting with circumstance. "This evasion of responsibility leads to self-deception, futilities, failures, blindness to opportunity for greatness and nobility."[56]

Fourth, there is an aspect of evil that we experience as

loneliness. This loneliness often arises because of acceptance of conventional experience and hiding our original selves from others.

Thus, the evil that we experience and from which we need to be saved has four aspects: inner conflict, futility or meaninglessness, guilt, and loneliness. "To know oneself with a minimum of illusion and error is a mark of advanced maturity."[57]

Finally, built into the nature of the world are various hierarchies, for example, of perception, of talent, and of ability. Some of us are more limited than others in our appreciative abilities and our creative possibilities. This is part of the tragic dimension of life.[58]

Hope

Humanity is not without hope precisely because there is the creativity at work within each person that is greater than oneself. This creativity drives us toward mutuality and caring. "It is this constant outreach, this sense of dependence, this striving to become organically united with something outside oneself that makes one religious."[59] Furthermore, "commitment to some greatest is the deepest need [in a normative sense] of human nature."[60] The "greatest" is creativity, and it is able to satisfy humanity's need once an individual is committed to it. Consequently, "the human problem is to shape human conduct and all other conditions so that the creative event can be released to produce maximum good."[61]

The task for humankind is to meet the conditions that creativity demands. "(U)nless a person sees and accepts one's destiny as servant and material for the progressive creation of the world—creation of meaning—the age of supertechnology is the age of doom."[62] Wieman's position is summarized in *The Intellectual Foundation of Faith*: "According to this understanding of the human situation we find our salvation, our deepest satisfaction and our fullest actualization of potentialities in a creativity which operates in our own personality, in society and history to reconstruct the world in such a way as to expand our horizons in the four fold ... [creative event]."[63]

And if we give ourselves in the wholeness of our being "to the power which creatively transforms when one commits oneself to it, and when other required conditions are present, the meaning of life is not lost and hope and courage do not fail."[64]

In summary, each human being has great potential to do good and to promote creative good. But each also has inherent limits and encounters limitations in the world, some of which she or he must overcome and some which he or she must accept.

We now turn to the doctrine of salvation and the nature of this necessary commitment to creativity.

Salvation

"Courage and zest for living at the human level can be had only by finding ultimate security in creative transformation itself."[65]

In the discussion of human nature, we have seen that

Wieman believed that humans are in need of radical transformation whereby we recover an "original self." Then we are able to live more fully in the sense of growing in appreciative consciousness.[66] A person is saved when creativity becomes that person's ruling commitment; with this ruling commitment there is an increase of value, of qualitative meaning, and of the growth of connections of appreciable activity. Life is lived with a continuing richness of felt quality that is impossible otherwise.

The moral law that issues from creative interchange might be stated thus: "Act in every situation in such a way as to provide conditions most favorable for creative communication and appreciative understanding among all parties concerned."[67]

Thus, salvation means more than the increase of value for the individual. Salvation, in Wieman's view, reaches out to "all parties concerned" and has social or corporate consequences. It involves efforts to "reconstruct the world."[68] When one has given oneself over to the ruling creativity, one is engaging in a process that promotes the increase of global unity and societal renewal. Wieman's soteriological concern focuses on the individual involvement in creative events, but the consequences reach toward a whole new earthly order, a City of God on earth.

Before discussing what salvation is for the individual and for society, we shall first look at how one finds it.

Preconditions

First, Wieman affirms that one must recognize that one is in a human moral predicament, that one does frequently do what one does not want to do, that one truly is in need of transformation and salvation, and that this salvation does not come from oneself alone.

Second, persons are required to provide necessary conditions for the working of the creativity that has the power to transform us as we cannot transform ourselves.[69]

With regard to the first matter, the moral predicament in which humanity finds itself arises from three conditions. First, persons oftentimes, as self-conscious creatures seeking to protect themselves, distort their evaluations of themselves and others both consciously and unconsciously. Consequently, intuitions are often in error, and the creative insight is impaired. Second, there are distortions that arise because of the community and culture in which one lives. Such narrowed vision, prejudice, bias, or other distortion is particularly dangerous and often leads differing communities into conflict. Third, humankind is in a transition state, and we are not what we could become; we are unstable and hence do not have the psychic organization that enables us to make complete and accurate judgments.[70]

After recognizing one's shortcomings, one must also practice rituals of personal commitment. Wieman is concerned that we achieve a state of wholeness or integration such that we will have healthy-minded intuitions that can guide conduct in a way that is conducive to further creative transformation.[71] Thus, "the second requirement is the practice of personal commitment by which the self is unified under a ruling devotion and one's resources most fully brought into action."[72]

This involves, first of all, finding a vocation that enables one to develop one's talents and potentials to their greatest extent. Wieman notes that this is a highly individual task, but adds that the vocation should have as its aim the transformation of humanity. This vocation is (1) to be fitted to the individual, and (2) to add to providing conditions necessary for continued human transformation.

In addition to finding one's vocation, one should give oneself completely in one's devotion to creativity. Wieman states this succinctly: "When one not only accepts oneself for what one is but [also] gives oneself as one is in the wholeness of one's finitude with a devotion not diminished but magnified by failure, guilt, and error, one lives with a magnified power of action, with a more reliably discriminating judgment concerning good and evil."[73]

Finally, in Wieman's program there must be an intensity and a persistence of commitment. These practices will be different for different persons. Wieman wrote about his own way in *Methods of Private Religious Living*. In any exercise the goal is to unify the self for action, to attain that reorganization that will have right intuitions, and to join oneself with the most important reality that there is. The most important reality is the creative transformation of humanity that is going on in human history.[74] And, the "goal of personal commitment is to bring about this creative transformation of the self and like transformation in others."[75]

Fruits of Commitment

What is the result of this personal commitment? Wieman responds: "This reorganization of the conscious and unconscious levels of the human being is the greatest good to be sought because (1) it is triumphant over the ... [evil] realities, (2) it enables one to act effectively under the guidance of reliable intuitions, (3) it unifies the self so that all the resources of your life can be brought into action, (4) it satisfies the wholeness of your being as nothing else can do."[76]

This in some detail is Wieman's proposal by which the individual finds salvation. What it involves is a commitment to a power, God, that is not fully known and a commitment to continue to search out and to provide the necessary conditions for creative events. It is a dual commitment requiring a religious faith and the continued increase in knowledge as elements of our cooperative activity. It is both a surrender to God's creativity and a commitment to personal effort to further God's creativity.

Wieman summarizes this dual commitment in *The Growth of Religion*: "As long as human life shall endure, the only way of deliverance and the only way of abundance for us will be this: Absolute commitment to the total goodness of God before one knows what it is, and then finding this good progressively by intelligent action and sensitivity of response in each concrete situation."[77]

Justice

The concept of "the Kingdom of God" is important for Wieman's thought.[78] (I shall speak of the triumph of God in order to avoid feudal imagery.) As already noted, one of his predominant concerns is a soteriological one in which the world is brought to progressively higher levels of global community and qualitative meaning. Through the transformation of individuals, the world is progressively enriched and brought closer together. The goal is justice, a world that will be ruled by a dominant commitment to creative interchange.

At one point, he describes the triumph of God as an association of communicating personalities.[79] And, he states, "the creative relation between human beings should be made central . . . if we are to find the way of salvation from degradation and dehumanization."[80] Wieman also states, "The . . . [triumph] of God is a world so transformed that every part responds with rich delivery of meaning to every other part and supremely to the spirit of humanity."[81]

Wieman expresses his concern for societal transformation in many of his works and analyzes the need for structural changes. He proposes the future shape of industry and such institutions as education, government, and the church if they were under commitment to creativity.[82] In addition to individual commitment to creative transformation, the realization of God's triumph throughout society requires (1) a widespread recovery of sensitivity in an age of science that has tended toward reductionism, (2) an increase of symbolic communication, (3) a recovery of small group associations, and (4) education for creativity.[83] Although Wieman did not develop a doctrine of the church in great detail, we shall see how these and other suggestions contribute to such a doctrine in a powerful way.

Salvation and the City of God are clearly of this world. We shall save Wieman's concept of meaning in history for our discussion of his eschatology. Salvation involves a restoration of wholeness of the individual in community and with it comes the "victory over sin, death, the devil, the curse, and the law and the gift of eternal life."[84] By this, Wieman means that we overcome our limits because we thus find freedom to act to further creativity in this world. The individual's appreciative consciousness is enhanced and good (value) is increased because of the increase in the formation of connections of mutual support, mutual control, and mutual facilitation between appreciable activities.[85]

The Challenge

In Wieman's thought, it is each person's duty (and ability) to provide conditions that will enable continued and progressive human transformation. It requires the dual commitment discussed above (1) to God as Creative Event and (2) to increasing knowledge.

And it is not easy. It is not possible to know with certainty that God will respond. That is, creative transformation may not occur every time one believes one has provided the necessary conditions. This is necessarily true because of his process metaphysics. No two situations can ever be the same; conditions required for creative transformation will be different, sometimes subtly and of little consequence, but sometimes appreciably with major impact. Thus, one needs continually to seek out what is required of oneself. This is not to deny that one can learn from one's past; it simply means that constant diligence is necessary.

To summarize: The salvation that Wieman discusses requires that each person provide necessary conditions for creative interaction. Nonetheless, humankind does not save itself. God (Creativity) is a sovereign power that transforms humans through progressive creation. The ultimate goal and challenge to pursue is the triumph of God as Creativity, which then becomes dominant in societies as well as in individual lives.[86]

"...the greatest fulfillment in anyone's life comes after one's death in the lives of one's children or friends and associates, or in some institution one has served or in some other development of life which one has promoted."[87]

Christology

Before 1939 Wieman, for the most part, was reluctant to employ Christian language. There were exceptions, however, when he moved from philosophical analysis to theological discourse, and then he made statements such as the following:

> This way of salvation can be described as accepting Jesus Christ as our only Lord and Master.... Jesus Christ becomes the only way of salvation when one recognizes (1) that Christ stands for a total good that is indefinitely richer, higher, deeper than any specifications we are able to set up; and (2) that Christ stands for that way of life in which the only sovereign control is the uncomprehended will of God, to be sought in each situation with utmost sensitivity and intelligence.[88]

His article, "Some Blind Spots Removed," marked a change, at least temporarily, in his thinking about Christian language and Christian symbols.[89] And in particular in *The Source of Human Good*, Wieman writes about the Christ event and Jesus' role in it with great feeling and sensitivity. Wieman's christological position appears most clearly in his statements in this book.

As noted above, Jesus the man is not to be confused with the process of creativity at work in the world, even though his life and teachings may have been a precondition for its working. The Christ event for Wieman centers around the community of love and fellowship that grew up among the disciples after Jesus' death. In the fellowship about Jesus there arose a "complex creative event."[90] There was a "miraculous mutual awareness and responsiveness toward the needs and interests of one another."[91]

Wieman spells out how the fourfold creative event characterized what happened to the disciples. With Jesus' crucifixion there was a breaking down of the dominant Hebrew perspective that anticipated a Messianic King who would rule over an earthly Kingdom of God.[92] With the "resurrection" the disciples were able to undergo transformation by creative interchange that went "beyond the bounds of their cultural heritage."[93] It was the creative power, the creative event of transformation and not the man Jesus that arose from the dead.[94]

In *The Source of Human Good*, Wieman speaks of salvation through Jesus Christ and explains it as the transformation in the life of a person when that individual shares in the same kind of relationships and self-giving to creativity that the first disciples found at work among themselves.[95]

He also notes the importance of being a part of a religious tradition and argues that one cannot be religious in general. Christ alone is our salvation "in our tradition" by which he means the Christian community to whom he is speaking.[96] Even in his final book, *Religious Inquiry*, he still maintains that the best way to understand the creativity at work is to identify it with Jesus Christ.[97] "But to say that we alone have the saving faith of the world is not a warranted statement."[98]

Thus, the creative event finds its paradigmatic, but not exclusive, expression in the resurrection event in which the disciples were transformed. Wieman takes the view that "something happened" to the disciples, namely creative transformation. They memorialized and attempted to capture the richness of the event through the narrative stories of post-Easter appearances. Jesus, the man from Nazareth, initiated or catalyzed a creative event that has reached around the world in its consequences. Christ is illustrative but not solely constitutive of the creative event.

The living Christ is quite separate from Jesus. Rather it is "the domination by the creative event over the life of a person in a fellowship made continuous in history."[99] And the living Christ continues to have human salvation as the focal point. "Indeed, when 'Christ' is identified with the way of life revealed in the fellowship of Jesus, we find therein that creativity which expands the activities of mutual support across conflicts and diversities."[100] The revelation of God continues in ongoing creative events inspired by the Christ event, for example, the fellowship of the disciples and the church at its best today. For Wieman, the Christ event has been the clearest, most powerful symbol within the Western heritage by which humans may come to know the power of creative transformation for themselves.[101]

Eschatology and the Meaning in History

Eschatology, in the traditional sense of "last things" or "the end of time," does not play a central role in Wieman's thought. It goes against his empirical bias for him to speculate about the end of time, about time beyond time, or about the triumph of good over evil in ultimate terms. Final or ultimate outcomes are beyond our knowledge.[102] Wieman much prefers and insists that we must look to the creative event within history in order to find grounds for hope. The human mind is created in history, and therefore it does not make sense "to talk about any kind of human experience beyond history."[103]

For Wieman, history is the supreme achievement of the creative event.[104] In history humankind may reach new heights of appreciative awareness and community. History finds its meaning in the creative transformation of human minds.[105]

Wieman believes that there has been progress in history, and he measures it in terms of a fourfold progression of (1) widening the upper levels of the societal hierarchy to include more people, (2) increasing the diversity of intercommunication among individuals and groups, (3) each person apprehending more of the meaning that others have to communicate, and (4) each person integrating more of these

communications into his or her own life and personality.[106]
Although progress may have waxed and waned at different times, it has been dominant over the long run. This is
humanity's prime source of hope. He emphatically states
this saying, "The hope of women and men lies in a cumula-
tive development through history, and human good can only
be increased by progressive accumulation of good through
a sequence of generations."[107]

Wieman, as noted above, does not believe in the final
triumph of good over evil or the transmutation of evil into
good at the end of time by a beneficent omnipotent deity.
"Not all the values are conserved. Not all that are worth
conserving are preserved."[108] Nor does Wieman seek to find
the highest values in the structure of the universe. The universe is progressively created and undergoes transformation relative to our knowledge.[109] Moreover, there is a good
possibility, according to Wieman, that the infinite universe
is not one coherent system.[110] He also holds out the bleak
yet honest possibility that: "if we decide for creativity we
must accept the fact that creativity is not omnipotent. It
might fail. It may sometime come to an end.... Any attempt
to make final predictions concerning the destiny of human
life endowed with creativity is foolish and futile, whether
the prediction be pessimistic or optimistic."[111]

In speculating about the ultimate end of life on this planet
with the death of the sun, Wieman is content with whatever increase of value may occur over the years. He concludes, "It will be a fact that on this planet God took on
existence to this degree."[112] The end. Goodbye! And it's
OK. How can we not accept it? Until then, let us add to

the value of the world by our co-creativity.

Wieman makes other, more positive eschatological statements at various points in his career. In *The Growth of Religion*, he states that to live by faith is to live "eschatologically." That means to "live for an uncomprehended totality of good which breaks into the world of human appreciation and purposive action unpredictably in the thronging fullness of concrete situations creatively emergent."[113] That is, there is an inbreaking of creativity into human living that is a ground for hope. "But it cannot rise triumphant until the breakthrough occurs in the lives of many associated individuals and continues more or less indefinitely."[114] This requires human cooperation, and therefore there are no final guarantees.

Wieman is even more optimistic in *The Source of Human Good*. He states his belief that affirmations regarding the triumph of good over evil are usually wishful thinking and that we must look to the evidence for whatever hope that there might be. For his evidence he selects the fact that qualitative meaning has increased in the world and has culminated in human life forms. He concludes that we have no knowledge that this process will cease. This is precisely opposite the final position he takes in *Intellectual Foundation of Faith* (1961).[115] It is apparent that Wieman in *The Source of Human Good* was allowing his wishes to supersede his philosophical consistency and his empiricism.

Again, in *Man's Ultimate Commitment* (1958), we can find Wieman speaking suggestively about eschatology in reference to creativity.

We cannot predict what creativity will bring forth in the life of humankind after millions of years, but there is much more reason to believe that creativity will save us at the last than there is reason to believe in divine intervention in any other form. They who believe in divine intervention at the end of history (called eschatology) admit they have no other evidence than a conviction of faith defended on the ground that it saves us from despair on the one hand and from self-destructive pride and cynicism on the other. But when God is identified with the creativity of history we have good reason to believe in a kind of divine intervention, if one wishes to use such words.[116]

Normally, Wieman does not wish to use such words. He is suggesting, however, that anyone who wishes to engage in such speculation about divine intervention in history or at the end of history is better off speaking in terms of a creativity that we know, rather than in any other terms.

Eschatology has validity for Wieman only in that such a doctrine points out greater possibilities for humanity within history, which we may then act upon. Daniel Day Williams poses the question to Wieman, "How can empirical theology anticipate that 'the triumph of creative good may be realized in history?'"[117] Wieman's response summarizes his position.

Nothing is known infallibly. Therefore we cannot be certain that creative good will triumph either in actual history or beyond history (whatever this may mean). But empirical theology opens the way for hope, because it can show that if creativity and its demands are accepted, it can and will transform human life toward the greater and deeper satisfactions of life, and save humanity from self-destruction and from mechanization of life which occurs when action is not inspired and guided by appreciation of individuality.[118]

But, this never "happens merely as a consequence of human striving to bring it about."[119] Creativity itself is supreme, and human hope lies in cooperating with this sovereign Creativity.[120]

The Church

Wieman discusses the role of the church throughout his writings, yet does not give it as much attention as he might have. He placed major emphasis on the role of educational institutions as agents that would have the power and ability to encourage creative interchange in human living and to foster knowledge of its primacy.[121]

However, in *Creative Freedom*, edited by Peden and Axel after Wieman's death, a stronger emphasis emerges clearly. In fact, the church, in promoting commitment to creativity, has an essential role to play if freedom and democracy are to be saved.[122]

The Church as Mystical Community

Some of Wieman's earliest statements about the role of churches or the institution of the church have a mystical orientation. In *The Wrestle of Religion with Truth*, the mystical strain appears as he discusses the religious vision which churchgoers share. Churches come into being because of the "common joy and the wonder that has befallen" a group of individuals.[123] Institutional churches with varying degrees of success have as their purpose the "mutual cultivation of religious vision."[124]

This mystical community does not deny the importance of the individual's relationship with God. In fact, one function of religion for the early Wieman is to inspire lonely intercourse with God.[125] Religion is extremely personal; it is something that "each person must find for oneself."[126] It involves living experimentally and taking risks as one seeks adjustment to God in worship. Although it is personal, it is not entirely private. Religion also functions to restore community even as solitude allows one to integrate one's experiences and to see oneself and the total community clearly. The church serves as a locus for the integrative process.

Church as Organic Fellowship

Wayne Shuttee in his valuable essay, "The Work of the Church," notes the development in Wieman's thinking about the church from a mystical community to an organic fellowship. The seeds of the concept of organic fellowship are evident in *The Wrestle of Religion with Truth*.

Each person, group, race, or age should be free to break away from the all-inclusive system, and within bounds produce chaos if need be, in order to make its own unique discoveries and develop its own peculiar potentialities. But these discoveries and developments cannot go far nor satisfy the individual most fully; and they will fail to make their full contribution to human living as a whole if they do not finally turn back into some sort of organized interchange and interaction with the rest of human life.[127]

Shuttee finds the concern for the fellowship of the church newly emphasized in *Methods of Private Religious Living* and in *The Growth of Religion*. What is involved is a "real transformation of personality ... through the creative interaction of the individuals involved."[128] The church is not necessarily an institutional church nor a local congregation, but is a transforming community.[129]

In *The Normative Psychology of Religion*, religion is "the endeavor to restore and preserve the health of the total personality and the social group."[130] The religious group should function to form a corrective philosophy that shall reconstruct the church as well as society. Although Wieman came to elucidate the social function of the church more fully, he is concerned at this stage of his thought with a creative fellowship that maintains and develops an enriching heritage of meditation and thought. He warns against institutional churches as reactionary and at points clearly prefers small, spontaneous creative groups.[131] But, later in *Now We Must Choose*, he states that the church provides reinforcement for the individual, and a means of propagating the committed life by bringing persons together under such circumstances that creative interaction can ensue most effectively.[132]

The organic fellowship has its paradigmatic form in the fellowship that arose in response to the work of Jesus and to his crucifixion. In *The Source of Human Good*, the fourfold creative event is elucidated in relationship to this group of disciples. A community of faith arose, a community committed to giving themselves to the creative event. It involved decisions (1) to live in such a way as to promote conditions favorable to the emergence of creative events, (2) to maintain associations with those committed to creativity, (3) to follow rituals that renew and deepen one's self commitment, and (4) to search out and confess, then repudiate, disloyalties to one's commitment.[133]

These kinds of decisions are necessary for the promotion of the creative event. In this connection Wieman states: "The primary duty of the church is neither mystical devotion nor trailing after other agencies in promoting social improvement. It is to demand insistently and everywhere that those human relations be provided between persons and between persons and nature which release the creative power of God."[134]

This kind of fervor implies, however, that the social role of the church is extremely important. It should lead, not follow. The call is for radical, immediate change rather than liberal gradualism.

This creative fellowship takes on soteriological import. For example, he states:

The church is the historic continuity of these means by which women and men may recover a renewed access to that way of life in which creative interchange dominates the life of humanity as it did in the fellowship of Jesus. The perpetuating symbolism and ritual may become a hollow shell, transmitting nothing of importance; but, even so, the vital significance and function of it can be restored. On that account it continues to be, even hollow and formal, *the most precious heritage of humankind,* for it is the means by which the creative event can again be lifted to dominate human devotion and command the complete self-giving of women and men to its saving and transforming power.[135] [italics added]

In *Man's Ultimate Commitment,* Wieman calls upon the church to assert its role as the institution that is to spread and deepen commitment to creative interchange. All institutions should come under a ruling commitment to creativity and should cooperate with one another.

But, "the very survival of the human race may depend upon some institution assuming the responsibility for the ultimate commitment of (all) humanity and not alone for a chosen few, which latter is what the church is now doing."[136] He is arguing for a universal commitment by churches to advance creativity. It is a prophetic call that the churches must undertake.

The distinctive function of the church centers around the nurturing of the gospel that proclaims the saving power of creativity when it has become dominant in individual lives and in community. The true church not only preaches this message, but exemplifies it in its own existence. Within the church grace "comes by way of the fellowship of those committed to creative interchange and through whom this creativity reaches to other people."[137]

Worship in the church is a fivefold process that brings creativity to dominance in individual lives and reaches out into the larger community.

- The institutional church upholds rituals and symbols that foster and maintain personal and group commitment.
- Serious self-examination is undertaken in order that one is able to acknowledge the unfaithfulness that occurs in every life.
- In common devotion there is social reinforcement and a deepening of the contagion of transformation and commitment.
- There is continued inquiry and instruction with regard to the nature and demands of the ultimate commitment.
- Finally, action arises out of involvement in these activities, and this furthers the elevation of creativity to a place of dominance in the lives of men and women.[138] Unfortunately, Wieman does not fully elaborate on the kind of action that arises.

With regard to the functions of the church, he also declares, "Liberating religion in contrast to all other kinds [of religion] has two outstanding characteristics. It practices ultimate commitment to creative interchange, generally under some other name such as God, Christ, or whatever; and it practices confession and repentance for any unfaithfulness to this commitment, thus preserving the integrity of individuals."[139]

In the creative fellowship, in the *koinonia*, symbols for worship will emerge that have meaning for the participants. If Wieman is not too concerned with revitalizing Christian symbols and language, it may be because he believes that new ones with contemporary meaning will emerge on their own when required conditions are met in the organic fellowship.

In Wieman's writings, there is a deep and unresolved ambivalence about the use of the traditional symbols of Christianity. He is intimately tied to his own tradition, but is acutely aware of and disturbed by its dogmatic claims, frequent shallowness, and conservative attachment to the status quo. Nonetheless, the traditional practice of meeting together for common worship and renewal is fundamental in Wieman's hopes for a better world.

The church, thus, is intimately bound with Wieman's soteriological concern. The human situation is reaching a desperate stage where the increase of power to destroy ourselves has not been matched with increased sensitivity and moral wisdom by which we will be able to exercise control over the vast destructive capabilities humanity now possesses.

The organic fellowship of the church not only serves the individual in one's quest for the abundant life under the domination of creativity, but also serves society and the world as an institution from which commitment to creativity may radiate, thereby progressively enriching the world.

The church is full of promise, but once again there are no guarantees. The church, with its ritual practices of commitment, its preaching and the symbolism of regular assembly, should develop in individuals and groups this commitment to creativity operating by way of creative interchange.

To the extent that the work of the church is effective, the moral striving of individuals and associations will be directed to providing social, interpersonal, and other conditions most favorable for the operation of this creativity in widening and deepening relations of mutual support and appreciative understanding between individuals, groups and peoples.[140]

The church has not always performed the task that Wieman identifies for it. But he believes that the church can recapture its vocation. And he believes that his analysis and description of creative events will help us to make the world a better place. Thus, his hope is that as we understand his insights we shall act upon them and become more deeply committed to creativity, which is a dual commitment to God and to personal and social transformation.

◆ ◆ ◆

"The mission of the church is to lead men and women to the full and free acceptance of human destiny with its hazards, its suffering, and its glory; also, it must lead women and men to strive to shape social institutions and the conduct of personal life in such a way that creativity can operate more effectively through the entire range of human existence."[141]

CHAPTER FIVE

Critical Responses to Wieman's Thought

Some have applauded Wieman's work as a creative contribution to Christian theology while others are more critical. Still others among the most orthodox reject entirely his empirical method and discount altogether the conclusions, hypotheses, and arguments that Wieman advances. The reasons are clear.

Wieman is in fundamental disagreement with most Christian doctrines of God. God is neither person nor omnipotent being, and this leads many to reject Wieman's conclusions about God and God's activity in the world. Also, although Wieman could conceivably speak of the triune nature of God (with creativity taking different forms as Father, Christ, and Holy Spirit) he does not do so.

Related to this is Wieman's understanding of Jesus, whose life, work, teachings, and death do not make him God. Jesus is not God's final revelation to humanity. His life was simply a precondition for God's acting in history in the complex Christ event in which creativity became dominant in the lives of the disciples. He is essentially Unitarian in his theology, and in 1949 he in fact became a Unitarian minister.

With regard to humanity, Wieman presents a balanced

picture of human nature and acknowledges that both evil and good are present. The way to salvation, which he occasionally symbolized as a commitment to Christ (as commitment to the dominance of creativity), is a process of human transformation. It is sparked by repentance and self-giving to creative interchange. There are many who will argue that Wieman does not do justice to Christianity with either this concept of salvation or his concept of God as creative event.

An eschatological hope that seeks salvation in history is at odds with much of traditional Christian thinking about a salvation at the end of time and existence beyond or outside of history.

The concept of the fellowship of the church has its parallels in Christian theologies of the more orthodox variety. Here Wieman's own Christian background emerges but once again transformed in his own distinctive manner.

Wieman believes that his theology preserves the best of Christianity while providing new concepts for the "modern mind." That which is preserved is (1) God's revelation of Himself in Christ, (2) the forgiveness of sin through personal transformation, (3) salvation, and (4) God's supremacy over and priority before created goods.[1]

Thus, in Wieman's theology there are continuities with a more orthodox brand of Christianity. But he goes far beyond orthodoxy in his empirical approach which counsels exploration, revision, openness, and critical thinking in order to be compatible with modern, scientific understandings of the world. In his philosophy of religion Wieman has achieved an interlocking system of thought which translates into a coherent natural theology. In doing this, he accepts major discontinuities and radical disparities that he does not attempt or want to reconcile with Christian dogma or tradition.

Specific Criticisms

Wieman correctly perceives the major criticism leveled against him. In his concern for history and the progressive domination of the world by a transforming creativity, Wieman is accused of ignoring both cosmological and ontological analyses, which are necessary to provide a more complete picture of the human condition, of God, and of the world. In this view, a broader metaphysics is necessary in order to respond to human needs and questions. Such statements require the use of analogical inference, which Wieman avoids, if not rejects.

Randolph Crump Miller states that "Wieman refused to make use of both analogy and metaphysics and therefore never got beyond a barren creativity."[2] His naturalistic materialism limits his ability to make inferences.

Daniel Day Williams, as well as Robert Calhoun and Charles Hartshorne, has also criticized Wieman for his analogical omissions.[3] According to their way of thinking, he did not go far enough with the theologian's task of symbolizing and was interpreting experience too narrowly. With the same concern, J. Kuethe asks whether such a minimal definition of God as Wieman offers is actually trustworthy.[4]

Miller sums up this issue by arguing that Wieman is too

precise in his empirical claims and limits God as God is actually known.[5] Many assert/know/feel that they "know" God in greater depth than Wieman argues is possible. Herein lies a basic epistemological difference, and Miller faults Wieman, arguing that his metaphysical presuppositions unduly restrict the conclusions that may be drawn.[6] John Macquarrie similarly declares "The End of Empiricism" as a philosophical method that has been undermined more by the critiques of philosophers of science than anyone else.[7] Similarly, but using logical analysis, Nancy Frankenberry questions the rigor of Wieman's empiricism (although affirming the heuristic value of Wieman's approach).[8]

Others have criticized Wieman for his empiricism arguing that it is in fact a veiled idealism with its emphasis on creativity as a universal in human experience. Meland suggests that Wieman never escaped Hocking's influence.[9] J. A. Martin also criticizes the Platonic tendencies in Wieman's empiricism and materialism.[10] In addition, Martin correctly questions Wieman's linguistic and conceptual clarity in his earlier works.[11]

Finally, congruent with some of the above, others have criticized Wieman's empiricism because of the ambiguity between the experience that Wieman outlines on the one hand and Christian tradition and biblical witness to God's activity on the other. The question posed is, "If Wieman's empiricism reflects what is actually going on in the world, why is it not immediately embraced? That the creative event was at the root of what happened around Jesus and to the disciples is far from obvious."[12]

Wieman's Response

Wieman is correct to think that the major criticisms of his thought bear on his failure to speak either cosmologically or ontologically beyond history. These attacks are in many respects leveled because Wieman is said to delineate experience too narrowly and too literally. By way of response, Wieman readily admits that experience is infinitely richer than we can know. His method simply prohibits him from claiming more than we can know and from claiming that symbols have unquestionable truth value beyond their expressive, emotive value. Wieman defends his position, stating: "For the sake of the infinite, if you wish to put it that way, or to keep ourselves faithful to the demands of cosmic possibility, if your theology prefers that expression, we must first of all commit ourselves to what alone can give us whatever glimpse we may ever gain of these demands. That means that we must commit ourselves to the creativity which expands and deepens our vision of that infinite context in which we conduct our lives."[13]

Wieman holds firm to the belief that all knowledge, religious or otherwise, must find verification in experience and that the scientific, empirical method is the best means that we have for discussing the nature of the reality in which we live, including the reality of God.

To those like John Macquarrie who suggest there are other ways of obtaining knowledge, Wieman would simply disagree. Moreover, Wieman's brand of empiricism not only withstands most of Macquarrie's other arguments, but also anticipates his concerns. For example, when

Macquarrie invokes Buber and a notion of "relational" knowledge of persons through "participation or communion," Wieman of course concurs in the fundamental importance of such experiences. However, he would argue that these experiences, as important as they are, do not produce "knowledge."[14] He continues to insist on the distinction between the analytic and the emotive experiences and on a narrow definition of knowledge.

Wieman respects the use of symbols that convey the rich, felt quality of immediate experience and that tie experience of past and present together into meaningful wholes. But with regard to his lack of symbolic language, he responds directly. He simply has not chosen for himself the task of revitalizing Christian tradition, symbol, and myth through a detailed translation in terms of creative events. He does employ such a method of correlation in making christological statements, but does not expand upon it.

With regard to the life of worship and devotion, Wieman offers the following prayer, which illustrates some of the criticism and typifies Wieman's own usage:

Take us into the depth of creative interchange
with its peace and power and love and wisdom.[15]

Wieman, for his part, rejects the methodological approaches of most other theologians because they make claims about God that Wieman believes cannot be substantiated. In *Religious Inquiry*, Wieman attacks, among others, Barth, Tillich, and Whitehead for their respective biblical, ontological, and cosmological approaches. He admires

Barth's emphasis on the actions of God within history, but rejects his thought for its failure to test biblical truths by the use of reason. Wieman also admires Tillich and his understanding of the power of noncognitive symbols. He also believes that Tillich is correct when he concludes that the central religious problem is that of human finitude. But he finds the ontological focus inadequate to discuss salvation because it is removed from everyday experience. Although Wieman also acknowledges his debt to Whitehead, he rejects his cosmic speculation.[16]

Given the radically differing presuppositions and/or conclusions about epistemological method and religious expression, these criticisms of Wieman and his responses are inevitable. Barth's neo-supernaturalism is impossible to reconcile with the modern age. Tillich as a pietistic liberal affirms both a nature/spirit dualism and posits a nonhistorical God in the form of Being itself, an approach untenable at least from a historicist perspective. And Whitehead, while monistic rather than dualistic, is similarly found lacking from the historicist perspective that affirms only a God in history and resists speculative rationalism.[17]

The critiques of Wieman's thought center on epistemological differences and the adequacy of Wieman's descriptions of God to do justice to (1) experiences of God, (2) the needs of daily religious life and worship, and (3) the intellectual needs of some for more comprehensive metaphysics. Wieman, however, continued to affirm that an empirical method such as he attempted was the best one to employ, notwithstanding, and perhaps because of, its necessary limitations.

CHAPTER SIX

Wieman and Contemporary Theologies

Wieman's primary concern has been the intellectual and philosophical task of providing and advancing a concept of God as creative event. Ultimately he has chosen the philosophical job of promoting conceptual clarity and not the theological one of enriching the life of worship and religious practice. Wieman provides the intellectual foundations for a naturalistic faith that will be responsive to those who are living in a secular culture dominated by a scientific world view and who are critical of ancient supernaturalisms. By casting God in terms of an actual ongoing creative process that appears in human lives, Wieman is hoping to make God a part of the available believable once again.

Wieman is fully aware that religion and worship spring out of a culture and that being religious in general is next to, if not totally, impossible. What he seeks is a renewal of the central notion of the Jewish-Christian concept of deity who works immanently in history. He uses the language of creative events to reflect the concept of God acting in history and rejects the notion of a God who is transcendent in the sense of being beyond space and time; that latter kind of God will not reach us in our daily living. But he retains

God's transcendence inasmuch as the creative process/creativity is greater than humanity.

Wieman also respects mystical experience and retains the concept of God who engages us in the fullness of time. In these moments humans find themselves enriched and transformed. Yet, Wieman always refuses to accept mystical experiences as sources of knowledge until they have been subjected to scientific testing. This is the only way to know the validity of one's intuitions and to act responsibly. And for Wieman humanity has reached a stage where we cannot afford to act irresponsibly.

Wieman, of course, has his own minimal process metaphysics of creativity, yet he finds little reason to speculate broadly. In his approach, to expand God-talk to include analogical inferences does not increase knowledge. Moreover, such language may be and often is positively confusing and otherwise detrimental. In his rebuttal to his critics, he is simply stating that he believes that his approach, by its thoroughgoing and self-limiting empiricism, is the best one he is aware of based on his own experience. This approach, he believes, has value—soteriological value—for humankind now and in the future. As a pragmatic matter, Wieman believes other methods are not as useful.

His influence on theologians such as Daniel Day Williams, Bernard Meland, and Bernard Loomer was extensive, although none adopted as strict an empirical method. Also in terms of Wieman's influence, it is of interest to note that Martin Luther King, Jr., wrote his doctoral dissertation at Boston University on Wieman's and Tillich's concepts of God. He criticized each and embraced the personalist philosophy of E. S. Brightman. Nonetheless, King's sermons are replete with themes and phrases that echo many of those of Wieman, particularly having to do with personal and social salvation.[1]

In the following sketches of several contemporary theologies, the common themes with Wieman's naturalistic theology emerge. The American pragmatic, prophetic tradition is alive and well, and Wieman's empirical theology can enrich and be enriched by each.

Toward Scientific Theology

Wieman believes that his approach will have particular importance as a worldwide community arises that is tied together by technology. The empiricism of modern science will spearhead a new Reformation, which he believes will reach around the world. With this development of worldwide community, which need not destroy particular cultures, there is the need for a new scientific theology that will lead to the dominance of creativity throughout the world. He states in *Religious Inquiry*: "Of all the innovations required to enable (women and) men to live at the high human level in the new age we are now entering, the one most critically important is the development of a form of religion which can join with science and morality to serve this creativity."[2]

Wieman's empirical process metaphysics, his realistic epistemology, his grounding in cognitive and interpersonal psychology as well as the evolutionary basis of his process approach commend his natural theology to an even more

broadly inclusive scientific theology. The natural philosophy of General Systems Theory is relevant to a scientific
theology with Wieman's empirical theology as a starting
point.[3]

Promising work has appeared in the writings of John
Ruskin Clark (*The Great Living System*) and the journal
Zygon. Numerous scientists have begun to write about their
theological conclusions, although some quickly lose their
empiricism in favor of grand speculations. Two of the more
rigidly empirical in intent are Freeman Dyson and James
Lovelock.

Freeman Dyson is professor of physics at the Institute
for Advanced Study in Princeton. In *Infinite in All Directions*, he expresses his conclusions about the meaning and
mystery of life based on his life's work as a scientist. Although he does not use the same language, his basic conclusion is similar to Wieman's, and like Wieman, he takes
an experimental attitude.

> My answers are based on a hypothesis.... The hy-
> pothesis is that the universe is constructed according
> to a principle of maximum diversity. The principle
> of maximum diversity operates both at the physical
> and at the mental level. It says that the laws of na-
> ture and initial conditions are such as to make the
> universe as interesting as possible. As a result, life is
> possible but not too easy. Always when things are
> dull, something new turns up to challenge us and to
> stop us from settling into a rut. Examples of things
> which make life difficult are all around us: comet

impacts, ice ages, weapons, plagues, nuclear fission, computers, sex, sin and death. Not all challenges can be overcome, and so we have tragedy. Maximum diversity often leads to maximum stress. In the end we survive, but only by the skin of our teeth.... To this process of growth and diversification, I see no end. [4]

Admittedly, such a hypothesis and vision may seem even less poetic than Wieman's and much more austere.

James Lovelock's development of the Gaia hypothesis, on the other hand, is significant in that it includes a mythopoetic dimension that any theology, and especially a scientific theology, must have if it is to be useful in strengthening and articulating faith and commitment. As already noted, Wieman emphasized the importance of worship and the rituals of commitment but did not himself do much to articulate creativity or the creative event symbolically. The Gaia hypothesis seeks to reflect a scientific understanding of the world/universe but includes reverence toward and soteriological emphasis on the creative, homeostatic complexity of the planet Earth. While arguing against any anthropocentric bias or preeminence of the human species, the Gaia hypothesis nonetheless calls upon human initiative and responsibility. Still the subject of considerable debate as a matter of scientific accuracy, the Gaia hypothesis may point the way to a new scientific theology not at all antithetical to Wieman's concerns. (Rosemary Radford Ruether's *Gaia and God: An Ecofeminist Theology of Earth and Healing* is a quite different approach that seeks to reclaim the legacies of Judaism and Christianity and embraces the Gaia metaphor.)

Randolph Crump Miller addresses himself to the question of a modern, scientifically grounded theology.

> If we are seeking for a theological position that commends itself to the twentieth century scientific-minded person, we may do well to start with experience, see that certain concepts work satisfactorily and place the thought system within the framework of a metaphysics. There is a sense in which any philosophy is a vision which appeals to self-evidence rather than proof. In light of experience one responds to suggestions that become self-evident; then one returns to various experiences with the concepts that are developed.[5]

Although Miller and Wieman disagree regarding the utility and necessity of metaphysical speculation and analogical inference, we can see that Wieman has done exactly what Miller suggests. Wieman's concept of God as creative event became self-evident to Wieman in the sense that Miller describes. Wieman then went about interpreting experience in terms of creative events.

Finally, the task of developing a scientific theology is grounded on the premise that a scientific worldview is gradually spreading across the world and radically changing the traditional conceptions of reality within many more traditional cultures. It also presumes, correctly I think, that science and religion are fully compatible and at least not antagonistic.

The difficulty that such an enterprise faces—and it may be intractable—is the tenacity of ancient religious myths that are deeply embedded in a culture, be they Jewish, Christian, Islamic, Hindu, Buddhist, or others. The incorporation of newer myth systems into the older is possible, and that is very much a part of the history of religions as they have evolved. Any such transformation, however, requires generations even in a technological age, and thus it will be a slow process.

An obstacle to this evolution is the reality that magical thinking is unlikely to be totally eliminated. More traditional religious approaches also offer a sense of stability and continuity whose appeal also increases as the rate of change in the world increases.

Wieman's vision, and he was a visionary, need not be given up, but he himself recognized the obstacles as far back as 1936. In contemplating the direction in which American religion might move, he identified the role of political and economic factors, "for these profoundly influence religious thought and life."[6] He suggested that religion will predominantly take the form of supernaturalism during periods of greater regimentation in public life and during those times when religion is fostered as a means of dealing with human need for comfort and security. On the other hand, "if we are moving toward a time when free inquiry and criticism shall be released, and the mind of humanity stimulated to search out all things by our natural powers, there will ensue the growth of a naturalistic religion that is conscious and professed." Furthermore, there is still another possibility. Our economic and political life may be entering a period neither of coercive regimentation nor of free inquiry, but of disorganization and increasing chaos. In that case dogmatic supernaturalism is almost sure to grow. Most likely, he believes, it is an oscillation between these periods with strong "surges and resurgences of supernaturalism."[7]

Part of the failure of empirical theology to capture the imaginations of many during the 1940s was a resurgence of supernaturalism. Liberal theology with its riskiness, its openness, and its tentativeness is not apt to fare well in a time of political crisis. With a change of mood and climate, however, these are times more conducive to free inquiry and criticism, and several other developments are noteworthy.

Creation-Centered Theology

One effort both to renew and to revise the theology and myths of a major world religion (Christianity) appears in the work of Matthew Fox and his colleagues who speak of a creation-centered spirituality/theology.[8] This project has many similarities with Wieman's naturalistic theology. Both Fox and Wieman emphasize the goodness of creation, creativity, compassion, the reality of suffering and evil, mutuality, community, personal transformation, and social reconstruction. Each speaks with urgency about the self-destruction of which humanity is capable and the necessity of religious commitment to prevent it.

Fox's fourfold path speaks of (1) befriending creation (*via positiva*), (2) befriending darkness, letting go and letting be (*via negativa*), (3) befriending creativity, befriending our divinity (*via creativa*), and (4) befriending new creation (*via transformativa*).

This approach has echoes of Wieman's fourfold creative event: increased awareness, integration of new meanings, expanded appreciations, and increased community. They are not identical, but they are mutually supportive.

Also like Wieman, Fox has both a modernist and mystical spirit. Although not as radically empirical in his method as Wieman, Fox turns to science to develop a modern cosmology. As one within the Christian tradition, he speaks of the Cosmic Christ in ways quite akin to Wieman's discussion of the Christ event. However, he adds a speculative metaphysics with his panentheism that Wieman's empiricism generally avoids.

Where Fox and his colleagues also make a significant contribution is their deep concern for (1) the development of rituals of worship and commitment and (2) the enhancement of personal, individual creativity. This work truly honors and promotes the creativity that Wieman explicates and celebrates.

Wieman might indeed welcome Fox's mythologizing of the scientific story of creation. In *The Source of Human Good*, Wieman writes, "Myth is a way of interpreting a complex event in which God has been intuited."[9] Myths help build community, contribute to a sense of meaning, are holistic and uniting, articulate a vision of the world, and vivify life's meaning.[10] Myth is "the subrational structure which is the substance, power and richness of a culture."[11]

Finally, while not previously mentioned in these terms, Wieman shares with Fox a dual commitment to beauty and justice.[12] For both Wieman and Fox, these two dimensions of human experience are integrally related and are goals for living. For Wieman, the concern for beauty and the good is most explicit in *The Source of Human Good*. Stephen Pepper goes so far as to assert, "Wieman is giving esthetic values a cosmic priority of status, and that his is an esthetic theory of God,"[13] which includes a call for social transformation.

In *Methods of Private Religious Living*, Wieman writes, "Beauty ... has awakened within us a yearning for the highest. Now is the time for the prophet to speak."[14]

This theme is even more pronounced in Fox's writings. Fox is explicit about the need for justice for all persons and speaks passionately about addressing the needs of the oppressed.

Robert McAfee Brown in his *Creative Dislocations of Grace*, states the relationship between beauty and justice in a way congenial to both Wieman and Fox.

How can beauty and the oppressed be understood together? For the Christian, the question is, How could they possibly be understood separately? So I conclude that concern for beauty is not a moral copout. It leads us firmly into the midst of all that is going on in our world. Where there is beauty apparent, we are to enjoy it; where there is beauty hidden, we are to unveil it; where beauty is defaced, we are to restore it; where there is no beauty at all, we are to create it. All of which places us, too, in the arena where oppression occurs, where the oppressed congregate, and where we too are called to be.[15]

Feminist and Liberation Theologies

Similarly, there are significant commonalities between Wieman's theology and contemporary liberation theologies. Certainly, Carter Heyward is right when she states, "White, straight, Euro-American men can speak only for themselves." And "theological truth [is emphatically contextual and] ... must be determined by those about whom and to whom it is meant to speak."[16]

Yet, Wieman's method and vision contain so many parallels with feminist and liberation theologies that some comparison cannot be ignored.

Admittedly feminist and liberation theologies have a breadth and depth difficult to summarize in detail. Even though generalizations about method or content must be limited, nonetheless certain features do define a "school" or movement. These elements include:

- a methodological starting point that honors the experience of individuals and groups who are
- oppressed (victimized, marginalized), yet
- who experience transformation (salvation) both
- as individuals and
- in community;
- whose empowerment occurs relationally (interpersonally) and

- often in dialogue with saving stories of a religious tradition and/or group heritage; and
- whose focus becomes this-worldly and justice-centered
- with an insistent sociological analysis of economic arrangements, class structure, and power relationships among and between groups.

In addition,

- God's energizing presence amidst the oppressed is celebrated, and
- contextual theology, which is very much within the American tradition of pragmatism, empiricism, and social analysis, replaces Anglo-European deductive, rationalist, idealist tendencies.

This description is by no means exhaustive, but from such an understanding of feminist and liberation theologies certain parallels emerge between these multifaceted, contemporary developments and Wieman's empirical theology.

First, with regard to method: Even though Wieman was thoroughly grounded in the rationalist, idealistic, Anglo-European school, he too rejected it for an experimental, empirical, contextual, pragmatic method. He was not a deductive systematician. He sought to identify God's active presence in the world and to name it clearly. Similarly, feminist and liberation theologies have a strong pragmatic, instrumentalist, and even empirical approach. Speculative metaphysics also tends to be at a minimum with an emphasis on God's action in history rather than on ontology or cosmology.

In many feminist liberation theologies and in Wieman's thought, we see not only similar methodological concerns but also kindred theological conclusions about

- deity which/who is transcendent, yet immanent both in history and in human relationships;
- God as process rather than person, symbolized in other than exclusively masculine terms;
- humanity's co-creativity, preciousness, and inherent dignity, as well as fallibility;
- salvation through transformation of self in this world, which arises relationally in community-based fellowship (of the church and/or small groups);
- salvation, which also arises in justice-centered activities; and finally
- renewal of worship, language, and religious practice.

When Carter Heyward speaks of religious vocation in terms of wisdom as perception of the wholeness of all that is; passion as immersion in the depth and breadth of the experiences of mystery, pain, and joy; justice as right relationships between and among people; and prayer as openness to the sacred, transforming reality of God,[17] then we may clearly see Wieman as a co-conspirator in the Spirit. Similarly, in both we hear the call to solidarity with those seemingly different from oneself, to mutuality, to co-creativity, and to resistance to and overthrow of narrow cultural conditioning. Together they also share commitment to the preciousness and dignity of persons combined with an awareness of interdependence.

With regard to God, Heyward states: "feminist theology moves in relation to a god who is relational (dynamic, changing, active). Like process theology, feminist theology recognizes this as true; unlike process theology, feminist theology presupposes no primordial and consequent bipolarity of natures in God...."[18]

Similarly, in looking at Cornel West's method and prophetic voice, at Starhawk's descriptions of holy mystery overcoming traditional authority, at Dorothee Soelle's embrace of mysticism and justice, at Latin American *communidades de base*, at South African liberation theologies, and at the experiences and writings of so many others, common elements with Wieman's empirical theology emerge. For Wieman, their common cause would be clear. The liberation that varying communities are now articulating reflects the process of creative interchange and aspires to the religious transformation of self and society that he promoted throughout his life.

On the other hand, while acknowledging certain kinship, the liberationists as a group would fault Wieman for his focus on salvation in interpersonal terms rather than transformation of social structures. He gives attention, but insufficiently so, to the structures of injustice, be they the evils of racism, sexism/patriarchy, heterosexism/homophobia, or economic exploitation. Wieman is acutely aware of the evils of materialistic culture, but he is far too optimistic about institutional transformation, particularly of industry.[19]

To be sure, Wieman identifies some of the problems of economic power and powerlessness, of institutional intransigence, and of social injustice. And he declares that social institutions must come under the guiding commitment to creative interchange. But for Wieman to say, as he does, that the "mission of the church is to lead men and women ... to strive to shape social institutions" is insufficient. Nor is it an adequate understanding of the evil that may occur through social systems to conclude that "the concentration camps of the Nazis and other evils of ... human history are the outward manifestations of this inner condition 'of the human heart,'" which is driven by "inner conflicts."[20]

Liberation theology challenges and augments Wieman with an insistent concern for analyzing social structures of injustice. In brief, liberation theologies tend to include a more highly developed and comprehensive social ethics and do great service by focusing on the particular situations of specific oppressed groups.

Wieman, for his part, might take issue with some of the nonempirical conclusions of some liberation theologies. Unlike those who speak of God's "preferential option for the oppressed," Wieman would argue that the evidence is equivocal at best. Certainly, this affirmation may be true of Jesus and his ministry. God was present in this motley crew. But this "preferential option" could not mean that God favors the oppressed (be they women, the poor, African Americans or whomever) in any historical or ultimate sense (whatever that means). The historical record repudiates any such suggestion. Wieman would encourage us not to underestimate the tragic dimensions of life, nor to engage in wishful thinking.[21]

But, if the affirmation of a "preferential option" means that God is vividly present in the ongoing liberation apparent in women's groups, elements of the black church, base-communities, lesbian and gay communities, and the like, then he would concur. Wherever creative transformation, empowerment, and vision lead to action and greater justice, then surely God is present. These are creative events, and thus holy.

A Final Question

One more issue arises as a question to Wieman from a feminist or liberation theology: Whose interests are being served by his approach to theology? What class, race, gender, or other interest group and/or community is benefiting?

The ideological component of any theology has rightly come under scrutiny by feminist and liberation theologians who pose this question.

With regard to Wieman, it is fair to say that he was conditioned by his times and also sought to engage in critical analysis of those ideas and events that transpired around him. Whether examining the thought of Whitehead in the 1920s or the existentialist philosophers or psychological theorists of the 1950s, Wieman not only turned to leading thinkers, but also engaged them in creative dialogue. But conditioned as he was, his understanding of the depth and breadth of the structures of oppression and of human suffering did not include many of the issues that are prominent today. Yet it is not hard to imagine him responding to and being transformed by these emerging new perspectives. It is true enough that he was never profoundly oppressed, given his life as a privileged, white, Anglo-Saxon, Protestant male, trained in elite universities, and a teacher primarily of the privileged.

Nonetheless, Wieman remained fundamentally faithful to the sovereignty of God in creativity and for the most part avoids idolatry. His commitment to creativity, to God, was a passion—a passion for justice.

CHAPTER SEVEN

A Prophecy and a Song

With regard to the comparative analysis, I am not arguing that there are any direct causal links between Wieman's empirical theology and the emergence of feminist and liberation theologies. But there is a common spirit and ancestry in the American pragmatic, empirical theological tradition, if not a direct lineage. Using Wieman's theology as a tool to understand a wide range of contemporary theologies is just that—one way to observe, understand, and to learn from these world-changing theological and sociological currents.

These new theologies help to sharpen an answer to a fundamental question for religious persons today, a question that also provoked Henry Nelson Wieman: "What is God saying? What is God up to? Where is God present in the world?"

God does seem to be up to something in feminist and liberation theologies. A passion for justice is stirring. In addition, it seems as if the dynamism of these theologies in their insistence on issues of justice reveals a divine presence that both threatens and challenges liberal theology.

The threat from feminist and liberation theology to liberalism is its radical stance against the structures of oppression that most religion implicitly supports in subtle and not so subtle ways.

Liberation theologies are "comforting the afflicted" by giving hope, strength, and power. But they are also "afflicting the comfortable," at least those who have some measure of moral sensitivity remaining within them.

The earlier question remains vital, not just toward Wieman's empirical theology, but to any approach: Whose interests are being served by your theological method and affirmations? What class, race, gender, or privileged interest group is benefiting?

Liberal religionists are generally at ease in Babylon despite a social activism that, for example, distinguishes Unitarian Universalists from all other religious groups.[1] Although perhaps expressing sympathy for the poor, there is a gradualist approach that borders on being a "preferential option for the status quo." Power is seldom shared, and the positions of privilege held by so many liberals often go unexamined. Fortunately, liberal religion in its openness to the new, its professed concern for prophetic action, and its inquiring spirit does still include some few who care passionately for a new day.

Wieman failed to capture the religious imaginations of the majority when reactionary neo-orthodoxy seduced so many. And the remythologizing of Christianity in terms of the Creative Event was not his self-appointed task. But he offers resources, as do feminist and liberation theologies, that can be taken up.

The need is great for cogent, naturalistic theologies that honor the intellect and critical spirit, that speak in symbols that touch the human heart and soul, that are self-critical, and that assist in the creation of a more just social order. God as creative event, or creative process, is trustworthy, vivifying, challenging, and redemptive, if we are loyal to it. Such a God still awaits our ultimate commitment.

At Home in Creativity

Henry Nelson Wieman's contribution lies in his theocentric emphasis on God operating in history in terms of empirical creative events. These moments of Creative Good, of Creativity, have the power to transform and to save humankind should women and men meet the required conditions. Fulfillment lies in a co-creativity that honors creation, human dignity, and human ability. As Daniel Day Williams noted, Wieman's penetrating insights and method spoke to liberal humanism in its own terms, restored an intellectually viable concept of God, and revitalized Christian theology for a generation of theologians.[2]

His thought enables some to embrace a specifically Christian theological reconstruction. For others, it is providing support for a modern, scientific theology, one which at its grandest proposes to lead to a new worldwide religious dialogue and possible reformation in the years to come.

Creation-centered approaches and various feminist and liberation theologies follow in the American empirical, pragmatic tradition. Wieman's natural theology provides a framework for understanding and appropriating some of their most important insights and, if nothing else, in the history of ideas marks the path of a sympathetic pre-

cursor. Furthermore, liberation theologies with their powerful social critique expand upon Wieman's analysis and
more clearly identify the creative event (God) as powerfully present in justice-oriented activity as well as in interpersonal connection.

Whatever direction one chooses, Daniel Day Williams
appropriately comments that "Dr. Wieman's way of point-
ing to the presence of God as the creative in experience is
the foundation of empirical theology."[3]

◆ ◆ ◆

The task of these pages has been to introduce Henry Nelson
Wieman and his work to a new generation. A major element has been to examine his philosophy of religion and to
render the implicit theological doctrines more explicit. Finally, his theological conclusions and method offer an approach that is still relevant in a world in which God so
often seems absent. God is present in our times in daily
events, instances of beauty, love, and justice. God is present
wherever creativity shines and thereby shapes the beloved
community.

Henry Nelson Wieman's witness to a God in creative
events has been consistent and eloquent. He has affirmed
human co-creativity with God, human preciousness, brokenness, and responsibility. He has sought to make the idea
and the practice of religious commitment to God—a God
that transforms and saves humanity, as we cannot do for
ourselves alone, when we meet the required conditions—
viable for the modern mind.

Wieman's single-minded emphasis on God's immanence, particularly in history, and on God's sovereignty, may not allow his position to be readily transferred into a theory of religion with universal applicability and appeal. Nonetheless, Wieman responded creatively to the cultural situation of his and our time—a time when science, technology, relativism, hedonistic materialism, and a this-worldly spirituality shape our globe and the lives of increasing numbers of people around the world.

Henry Nelson Wieman was a philosopher of religion, first and foremost. Attempts at conceptual clarification about God, a reality that Wieman believed to be operative as creativity in the world, dominated his work. Yet his ultimate concern was with the creative event, religious experience itself—creative growth with increased awareness, greater integration, new perspectives, and deeper community. The pursuit of truth and greater knowledge must always serve the increase of value, of the good, of justice. The fiery, analytic tools of reason are primarily employed for the transformation of self and of society.

God is not as hidden as we might think and feel. Wieman's purpose is to increase our sensitivity to the richness of felt-quality, new creation, which is always open to us within our experience. In this way, the world of matter becomes imbued with the spiritual. Material existence becomes spiritual as "things become expressive of human spirit."[4]

"Events cease to be material things merely and become a language, a prophecy and a song."[5]

◆ ◆ ◆

"If my home is in creativity itself, I can undergo great changes without despair."[6]

"Courage and zest for living at the human level can be had only by finding ultimate security in creative transformation itself."[7]

NOTES

Introduction

1. B. Meland, "Wieman's Philosophy of Creativity," in *Creative Interchange*, ed. J. Broyer and W. Minor (Carbondale, IL: Southern Illinois University Press, 1982), p. 21.

2. Cornel West, *The American Evasion of Philosophy* (Madison, WI: University of Wisconsin Press, 1989), p. 211 ff.

3. K. Cauthen in his *The Impact of American Religious Liberalism* (New York, NY: Harper and Row, 1962) does provide a brief and generally good synopsis of Wieman's thought. However, his treatment of Wieman's doctrine of the Church is inadequate. Other brief summaries include sections in R. C. Miller's *Empirical Theology—A Handbook* (Birmingham, AL: Religious Education Press, 1992) and in N.

Frankenberry's *Religion and Radical Empiricism* (Albany, NY: State University of New York Press, 1987).

Chapter One: Biographical Sketch

Opening Quotation: Henry Nelson Wieman, *Methods of Private Religious Living* (New York, NY: Macmillan, 1929), p. 154.

1. Wieman, "Intellectual Autobiography," in *The Empirical Theology of Henry Nelson Wieman*, ed. R. W. Bretall (Carbondale, IL: Southern Illinois University Press, 1963), p. 3. Had Wieman been writing today, I am confident that he would have used gender-inclusive language. Therefore, I have edited his words wherever quoted.

2. Wieman's publications include sixteen books, fourteen chapters in books by other authors, 102 articles in scholarly journals, numerous articles in the popular press, and two books of his writings edited by others either late in his life or posthumously.

3. Wieman, *Methods of Private Religious Living.*

4. See William S. Minor's *Introduction to Creative Interchange*, ed. J. Broyer and W. Minor (Carbondale, IL: Southern Illinois University Press, 1982), an invaluable collection of essays about Wieman's thought and relevance.

5. Wieman, "How I Got My Religion," *Religious Education*, 1931, 26: 841, quoted in H. Rosen, *Religious*

Education and our Ultimate Commitment, (Lanham, MD: University Press of America, 1985), p. 3. Rosen's book is another valuable contribution.

6. Wieman, *Methods of Private Religious Living*, pp. 185-186.

7. *Ibid*.

8. Buber, however, is not cited by Wieman as a primary influence.

9. Wieman, "How I Got My Religion," in Rosen, *Religious Education*, p. 3.

10. *Ibid*., pp. 3-4.

11. *Ibid*., p. 4.

12. Wieman, *Methods of Private Religious Living*, p. 195.

13. Wieman in *Empirical Theology*, ed. Bretall, p. 6.

14. Wieman, *The Organization of Interests* (Lanham, MD: University Press of America, 1985). Rosen, *Religious Education*, p. 5, and W. Minor, *Creativity in Henry Nelson Wieman*, (Metuchen, NJ: Scarecrow Press, Inc., 1977), p. 6.

15. Wieman, *Creative Freedom*, ed. Creighton Peden and Larry Axel (New York, NY: Pilgrim Press, 1982), pp. 105-106.

16. Wieman, *Religious Experience and Scientific Method* (New York, NY: Macmillan, 1926), p. 9.

17. Wieman, *Creative Freedom*, ed. Peden and Axel, p. 104 ff.

18. Wieman, "Theocentric Religion," in *Contemporary American Theology*, ed. V. Ferm (New York, NY: Round Table Press, 1932), I: 345.

19. B. Meland, "Wieman's Philosophy of Creativity," in *Creative Interchange*, ed. Broyer and Minor, p. 17.

20. Quoted by L. Axel in *Creative Interchange*, ed. Broyer and Minor, pp. 40-41.

21. L. Axel, "A New Turn in Religious Inquiry," in *Creative Interchange*, ed. Broyer and Minor, p. 37.

22. Wieman, *Religious Experience and Scientific Method*, p. 28.

23. H. Rosen, *Religious Education*, p. 7.

24. Wieman, *Methods of Private Religious Living*, p. 218.

Chapter Two: Wieman as Philosopher of Religion

Opening Quotation: Henry Nelson Wieman, *Methods of Private Religious Living* (New York, NY: Macmillan, 1929), p. 182.

1. Wieman, *Religious Inquiry* (Boston, MA: Beacon Press, 1968), p. 16.

2. W. Minor, *Creativity in Henry Nelson Wieman* (Metuchen, NJ: Scarecrow Press, 1977), p. 45.

3. Wieman, *Religious Inquiry*, p. 16.

4. Wieman and W. Horton, *The Growth of Religion* (Chicago, IL: Willet, Clark & Co., 1938), p. viii.

5. *Ibid.*, p. xiii.

6. Wieman, *The Source of Human Good* (Chicago, IL: The University of Chicago Press, 1946), p. 210.

7. Wieman, *The Intellectual Foundation of Faith* (New York, NY: Philosophical Library, 1961), p. 199.

8. W. R. Miller, *The American Spirit in Theology* (Philadelphia, PA: United Church Press, 1974), p. 76.

9. Wieman and Horton, *The Growth of Religion*, p. 246.

10. *Ibid.*, p. 238.

11. *Ibid.*

12. Wieman, *The Intellectual Foundation of Faith*, p. 199.

13. Wieman and Horton, *The Growth of Religion*, p. xiv.

14. Wieman, *The Intellectual Foundation of Faith*, p. 56.

15. *Ibid.*, pp. 56-57.

16. Henry Nelson Wieman, *Man's Ultimate Commitment* (Carbondale, IL: Southern Illinois University Press, 1958), p. 46; Wieman, *Religious Inquiry*, p. 4.

17. Wieman, *Religious Inquiry*, p. 139, and *The Source of Human Good*, p. 113.

18. Wieman, *Religious Inquiry*, p. 217.

19. Wieman, *Man's Ultimate Commitment*, p. 55.

20. Wieman, *Intellectual Foundation of Faith*, p. 4.

21. Wieman, *The Source of Human Good*, p. 103.

22. J. G. Kuethe, "Three Empirical Philosophies of Religion: Macintosh, Meland, and Wieman" (unpublished doctoral dissertation, Union Theological Seminary, 1963), pp. 66, 80.

23. J. Macquarrie, *Twentieth Century Religious Thought* (New York, NY: Charles Scribner's Sons, 1981), p. 187. Macquarrie places Wieman in a chapter on pragmatism under the subheading of "Protestant Empirical Modernists." Included with Wieman is Harry Emerson Fosdick, although Macquarrie by no means equates the two as theologians.

24. J. W. Bergland, "The Nature of Theological Inquiry in Henry Nelson Wieman," (Unpublished doctoral dissertation, Union Theological Seminary, 1972), p. 91 ff.

25. Wieman and Horton, *The Growth of Religion*, p. 258; Wieman, *The Source of Human Good*, p. 211; Wieman, *Man's Ultimate Commitment*, p. 138.

26. R. C. Miller, *American Spirit in Theology*, p. 10.

27. J. A. Martin, *Empirical Philosophies of Religion* (New York, NY: Columbia University Press, 1945), p. 107.

28. Wieman, "Intellectual Autobiography," in *The Empirical Theology of Henry Nelson Wieman*, ed. R. W. Bretall (Carbondale, IL: Southern Illinois University Press, 1963), p. 5.

29. Wieman and Horton, *The Growth of Religion*, p. 439.

30. Miller, *The American Spirit in Theology*, p. 16.

31. *Ibid.*, p. 195.

32. Wieman, *Methods of Private Religious Living*, pp. 46, 52.

33. *Ibid.*, p. 53.

34. Miller, *The American Spirit in Theology*, p. 95; Wieman, *The Source of Human Good*, p. 72.

35. Wieman, *Religious Inquiry*, p. 189.

36. Wieman, *The Source of Human Good*, p. 297.

37. *Ibid.*, p. 298.

38. *Ibid.*, p. 301. See Stephen Pepper, *World Hypotheses: A Study in Evidence* (Berkeley, CA: University of California Press, 1948), for a discussion of formism, mechanism, organicism, and contextualism.

39. Wieman, *The Source of Human Good*, p. 302.

40. *Ibid.*

41. Wieman, *The Directive in History* (Boston, MA: Beacon Press, 1949), p. 6.

42. *Ibid.*, p. 21.

43. Wieman, *The Source of Human Good*, p. 301.

44. Wieman, *The Directive in History*, p. 16 ff.

45. Wieman, *The Source of Human Good*, p. 302.

46. Wieman and Horton, *The Growth of Religion*, p. 386.

47. Wieman, *Religious Inquiry*, p. 12.

48. Wieman, *Man's Ultimate Commitment*, p. 81.

49. Wieman, *The Source of Human Good*, p. 200.

50. *Ibid.*, pp. 18-19.

51. *Ibid.*, p. 304.

52. *Ibid.*, p. 174.

53. *Ibid.*, p. 164.

54. *Ibid.*, p. 168.

55. *Ibid.*, p. 172.

56. Quoted in Miller, *The American Spirit in Theology*, p. 92.

Chapter Three: Wieman as Theologian

Opening Quotation: Henry Nelson Wieman, quoted in D. S. Harrington's *Outstretched Wings of the Spirit* (Boston, MA: Unitarian Universalist Association, 1980), pp. 107-108.

1. For background on these issues and period see: Sydney Ahlstrom, *A Religious History of the American People* (New Haven, CT: Yale University Press, 1972); *Creative Interchange*, ed. Broyer and Minor (Carbondale,

IL: Southern Illinois University Press, 1982); Kenneth Cauthen, *The Impact of American Religious Liberalism* (New York, NY: Harper and Row, 1962); *The Future of Empirical Theology*, ed. Bernard Meland (Chicago, IL: The University of Chicago Press, 1969); Randolph Crump Miller, *The American Spirit in Theology*, (Philadelphia, PA: United Church Press); and R. C. Miller, *Empirical Theology—A Handbook* (Birmingham, AL: Religious Education Press, 1992).

2. Meland in *Creative Interchange*, ed. Broyer and Minor, p. 21.

3. Wieman, "Reply to Burtt," in *The Empirical Theology of Henry Nelson Wieman*, ed. R. W. Bretall (Carbondale, IL: Southern Illinois University Press, 1963), p. 388; Wieman, *Religious Inquiry*, (Boston, MA: Beacon Press, 1968), p. 28.

4. Wieman, "Intellectual Autobiography," in *Empirical Theology*, ed. Bretall, p. 6.

5. Henry Nelson Wieman, *The Issues of Life* (New York, NY: Abingdon Press, 1930), p. 163.

6. Wieman, *The Source of Human Good* (Chicago, IL: The University of Chicago Press, 1946), p. 78.

7. *Ibid.*, pp. 58-69.

8. Wieman, *Man's Ultimate Commitment* (Carbondale, IL: Southen Illinois University Press, 1958), p. 4.

9. Wieman, *The Source of Human Good*, p. 65.

10. Wieman, *Creative Freedom*, ed. Creighton Peden and Larry Axel (New York, NY: Pilgrim Press, 1982), pp. 42, 69.

11. Minor, *Creativity in Henry Nelson Wieman* (Metuchen, NJ: Scarecrow Press, 1977), p. 184.

12. As reported by J. Bergland, Union Theological Seminary.

13. Miller, *American Spirit in Theology*, p. 25.

14. Wieman, *Religious Inquiry* (Boston, MA: Beacon Press, 1968), p. 193.

15. *Ibid.*

16. One of Kuethe's main conclusions in his "Three Empirical Philosophies" (see note 23 of Chapter 2) is that Meland has made a significant contribution to Wieman's thought because of Meland's concern for myth, worship, and poetry.

17. Daniel Day Williams, "Wieman as a Christian Theologian," in *Empirical Theology*, ed. Bretall, p. 85.

18. Wieman and Norton, *The Growth of Religion* (Chicago, IL: Willet, Clark & Co., 1938), p. xv; Wieman, *The Source of Human Good*, p. 263.

19. Wieman, "Intellectual Autobiography," in *Empirical Theology*, ed. Bretall, p. 6.

20. Miller, *American Spirit in Theology*, p. 125; Williams, "Christian Theologian" in *Empirical Theology*, ed. Bretall, p. 73.

21. Williams, "Christian Theologian," in *Empirical Theology*, ed. Bretall, p. 73.

22. B. Loomer, "Wieman's Stature as a Contemporary Theologian," in *Empirical Theology*, ed. Bretall, p. 392.

23. W. Horton, "God in Christ: Soteriology," in *Empirical Theology*, ed. Bretall, p. 185.

24. Wieman, *Religious Inquiry*, p. 195.

25. Georges Florovsky, "The Church of God," in *Empirical Theology*, ed. Bretall, p. 377.

26. Gustave Weigel, "The Paradox of Stable Change," in *Empirical Theology*, ed. Bretall, p. 349.

27. Wieman, "Reply to Weigel," in *Empirical Theology*, ed. Bretall, p. 372.

28. Wieman, *Religious Inquiry*, p. 51.

29. Wieman, "Reply to Burtt," in *Empirical Theology*, ed. Bretall, p. 388.

30. Wieman, "Reply to Horton," in *Empirical Theology*, ed. Bretall, p. 191.

31. Wieman, *Issues of Life*, p. 40.

32. On the other hand, David Lee Miller in "Buddhist Themes in Wieman's View of Creative Interchange," in Broyer and Minor's *Creative Interchange,* points to Eastern themes in Wieman's thought. Nancy Frankenberry in *Religion and Radical Empiricism* (Al-

bany, NY: State University of New York, 1987) also draws connections to Buddhist thought.

33. Wieman, "Intellectual Autobiography," in *Empirical Theology,* ed. Bretall, p. 18; Wieman, *Religious Inquiry*, p. 51.

34. Wieman, *Man's Ultimate Commitment*, p. 153.

35. Wieman, *Religious Inquiry*, p. 212.

36. Wieman, "Religion in Dreamland," *The New Republic*, 1926, p. 378.

37. Wieman, *The Source of Human Good*, p. 186.

38. Wieman, *The Directive in History* (Boston, MA: Beacon Press, 1949), p. 52.

39. *Ibid.*, p. 72.

40. Wieman, *The Source of Human Good*, p. 211 ff.

41. Wieman, *Man's Ultimate Commitment*, p. 51.

42. Wieman, *The Source of Human Good*, p. 51.

43. Wieman, *Man's Ultimate Commitment*, p. 153.

44. *Ibid.*, pp. 305-306.

45. Wieman, *The Source of Human Good*, p. 48.

Chapter Four: Wieman's Theological Doctrines

Opening Quotation: Henry Nelson Wieman, *The Source of Human Good* (Chicago, IL: The University of Chicago Press, 1946), p. 270.

1. *Ibid.*, p. 174.

2. *Ibid.*, p. 56.

3. *Ibid.*, p. 57. See also William Dean, *American Religious Empiricism* (Albany, NY: State University of New York Press, 1986), p. 31.

4. Wieman and W. Horton, *The Growth of Religion* (Chicago, IL: Willet, Clark & Co., 1938), p. 352.

5. *Ibid.*, p. 353.

6. *Ibid.*

7. *Ibid.*, p. 342.

8. *Ibid.*, p. 344.

9. Wieman, *The Source of Human Good*, p. 7.

10. Wieman and Horton, *The Growth of Religion*, p. 457; Wieman with Regina Westcott Wieman, *Normative Psychology of Religion* (New York, NY: Crowell, 1935), p. 51.

11. Wieman, *The Intellectual Foundation of Faith* (New York, NY: Philosophical Library, 1961), pp. 48, 104; Wieman, *Man's Ultimate Commitment* (Carbondale, IL: Southern Illinois University Press, 1958), p. 12.

12. Wieman, *The Directive in History* (Boston, MA: Beacon Press, 1949), p. 20.

13. Wieman, *The Wrestle of Religion with Truth* (New York, NY: Macmillan, 1927), p. 184.

14. In opposition to Whitehead, Wieman argues that the
    primordial nature of God is an order of creative en-
    ergy and is not a realm where structures of possibility
    await creation of a world in which they might have a
    place (Wieman, *The Source of Human Good*, p. 189).
    Rather, in creative events there is new creation that
    contains structures of possibility. God is always ac-
    tively creating reality and concomitant possibilities.
    Present levels of order are dependent on the possibili-
    ties within the prior levels. The "higher levels of ex-
    istence spring from, rest upon, and are undergirded
    by the lower" (Wieman, *The Source of Human Good*,
    p. 8). God is in no way passive as in Whitehead's pri-
    mordial nature. Order in creative events is intrinsic
    and comes from lower levels of creativity. It has a struc-
    ture and creates structures but is not imposed as in
    the Whiteheadian primordial order, which stores pos-
    sibilities until useful and relevant. He clarifies his re-
    interpretation of the primordial nature of God in his
    "Intellectual Autobiography" (in *The Empirical The-
    ology of Henry Nelson Wieman*, ed. R. W. Bretall,
    p. 9). In contrast to the consequent nature of God,
    which stores up all existence transforming and main-
    taining all value, Wieman sees the distinct possibility
    of irrecoverable losses of value. He believes that
    Whitehead's notion does not take seriously enough
    the power of evil, which Wieman characterizes as the
    obstruction of creative events and the destruction of
    qualitative meaning. (Wieman, *The Source of Human
    Good*, p. 193) We can see more clearly the divergence

from Whitehead in Wieman's thought as he moves to a focus on communication rather than cosmological speculation. These concerns come to the fore in *The Source of Human Good* and *Man's Ultimate Commitment,* although they are suggested in *Issues of Life* (New York, NY: Abingdon Press, 1930) in his discussions of the order of communication and progressive integration, which lead to the increase of human good and which sustain the movement of life toward the good. It is this understanding of communication and the order of love that becomes more fully developed as he explains the working of the creative event.

15. Wieman, *The Issues of Life*, p. 162.

16. *Ibid.*

17. Wieman and Horton, *The Growth of Religion*, p. 435.

18. Kuethe, "Three Empirical Philosophies of Religion: Macintosh, Meland, and Wieman" (unpublished doctoral dissertation, Union Theological Seminary, New York, NY, 1963), p. 232.

19. Wieman and Horton, *The Growth of Religion*, p. 351.

20. *Ibid.*, p. 359-363; Wieman, *The Intellectual Foundation of Faith*, p. 58.

21. Wieman, *The Source of Human Good*, pp. 7, 77-78, 264.

22. *Ibid.*, pp. 81, 193.

23. Wieman and Horton, *The Growth of Religion*, pp. 338-340.

24. Wieman, *The Wrestle of Religion with Truth*, p. 187.

25. Wieman and Horton, *The Growth of Religion*, pp. 364 ff., 383: God is "Father" as the power by which we are "brothers"; Wieman, *The Source of Human Good*, p. 282 ff.; Wieman, *Man's Ultimate Commitment*, p. 178.

26. H. Rosen, *Religious Education and Our Ultimate Commitment* (Lanham, MD: University Press of America, 1985), p. 58.

27. Wieman, *Intellectual Foundation of Faith*, p. 54.

28. *Ibid.*, p. 55.

29. Wieman, *The Wrestle of Religion with Truth*, pp. 138-139.

30. Wieman, *Intellectual Foundation of Faith*, pp. 52-55.

31. Wieman, *The Source of Human Good*, pp. 265-267.

32. *Ibid.*, pp. 81, 193.

33. See endnote 26; also, Wieman, *Normative Psychology of Religion*, p. 137.

34. B. Loomer, "Wieman's Stature," in *Empirical Theology*, ed. Bretall, p. 395.

35. Wieman, *Man's Ultimate Commitment*, p. 72.

36. Wieman, *Religious Inquiry* (Boston, MA: Beacon Press, 1968), p. 209.

37. J. Broyer, "A Final Visit with Wieman," in *Creative Interchange*, ed. J. Broyer and W. Minor (Carbondale, IL: Southern Illinois University Press, 1982), p. 86.

38. Wieman, *Religious Inquiry*, p. 135.

39. *Ibid.*, p. 114.

40. *Ibid.*, p. 10.

41. *Ibid.*, p. 179.

42. Wieman, *The Directive in History*, p. 70.

43. Wieman, *The Intellectual Foundation of Faith*, p. 8.

44. Wieman and Horton, *The Growth of Religion*, p. 458.

45. Wieman, *Creative Freedom*, ed. Creighton Peden and Larry Axel (New York, NY: Pilgrim Press, 1982), p. 59.

46. Wieman, *The Source of Human Good*, pp. 27-28.

47. *Ibid.*, pp. 106 ff., 125.

48. Wieman, *Man's Ultimate Commitment*, p. 10.

49. *Ibid.*, p. 109.

50. Wieman, *Normative Psychology of Religion*, p. 262.

51. Wieman, *The Directive in History*, p. 131.

52. Wieman, *Man's Ultimate Commitment*, p. 30.

53. *Ibid.*, p. 63; for a fuller discussion of evil see Wieman, *The Source of Human Good*, pp. 105-129.

54. Wieman, *The Source of Human Good*, p. 126.

55. Wieman, *Man's Ultimate Commitment*, p. 13.

56. *Ibid.*, p. 14.

57. Wieman, *Creative Freedom*, p. 67.

58. See Miller in *Creative Interchange*, ed. Broyer and Minor, p. 410.

59. Wieman and Horton, *The Growth of Religion*, p. 411.

60. *Ibid.*, p. 240.

61. Wieman, *The Source of Human Good*, p. 69.

62. Wieman, *The Directive in History*, p. 26.

63. Wieman, *Intellectual Foundation of Faith*, pp. 8-9.

64. Wieman, *Creative Freedom*, p. 42.

65. *Ibid.*, p. 45.

66. Wieman, *Man's Ultimate Commitment*, p. 10.

67. Wieman, *Man's Ultimate Commitment*, p. 32.

68. Wieman, *Intellectual Foundation of Faith*, p. 89.

69. Wieman, *Man's Ultimate Commitment*, p. 286 ff.

70. *Ibid.*

71. *Ibid.*, p. 286.

72. *Ibid.*, p. 290.

73. *Ibid.*, p. 292.

74. *Ibid.*, p. 294.

75. *Ibid.*, p. 295.

76. *Ibid.*

77. Wieman and Horton, *The Growth of Religion*, p. 487.

78. Wieman, *Religious Inquiry*, p. 137.

79. Wieman, *Issues of Life*, p. 221.

80. Wieman, *Man's Ultimate Commitment*, p. 157.

81. Wieman, *The Source of Human Good*, p. 272.

82. Wieman, *Man's Ultimate Commitment*, p. 163 ff.

83. Wieman, *The Directive in History*, p. 134.

84. Wieman, *The Source of Human Good*, p. 273.

85. Wieman and Horton, *The Growth of Religion*, p. 330.

86. Wieman, "Reply to Pepper," in *The Empirical Theology of Henry Nelson Wieman,* ed. by R. W. Bretall (Carbondale, IL: Southern Illinois University Press, 1963), p. 163.

87. Wieman, *Creative Freedom*, p. 97.

88. Wieman and Norton, *The Growth of Religion* (Chicago, IL: Willet, Clark & Co., 1938), p. 486.

89. Wieman, "Some Blind Spots Removed," *(Christian Century*, 1939), LVI: 116-118.

90. Wieman, *The Source of Human Good*, p. 41.

91. *Ibid.*, p. 39.

92. *Ibid.*, p. 227.

93. *Ibid.*, p. 43.

94. *Ibid.*, p. 44.

95. *Ibid.*, p. 276.

96. *Ibid.*, p. 287.

97. Wieman, *Religious Inquiry* (Boston, MA: Beacon Press, 1968), p. 194.

98. Wieman, *The Source of Human Good*, p. 287.

99. *Ibid.*, p. 269. Commenting on this paragraph, B. Meland states that Wieman's "theory of value was his alternative to a Christology," in *Creative Interchange*, ed. J. Boyer and W. Minor (Carbondale, IL: Southern Illinois University Press, 1982), p. 28.

100. Wieman, *Religious Inquiry*, p. 194.

101. Also see Rosen, *Religious Education and Our Ultimate Commitment* (Lanham, MD: University Press of America, 1985), pp. 58-66, and Marvin Shaw, "Naturalism and the Christ: Wieman's Christology," unpublished manuscript.

102. Wieman, *The Source of Human Good*, p. 92.

103. Wieman, *Man's Ultimate Commitment* (Carbondale, IL: Southern Illinois University Press, 1958), p. 273.

104. Wieman, *The Source of Human Good*, p. 307.

105. Wieman, *Man's Ultimate Commitment*, p. 266.

106. Wieman, *The Source of Human Good*, p. 123.

107. *Ibid.*, p. 11.

108. Wieman and Horton, *The Growth of Religion*, p. 320.

109. Wieman, *The Intellectual Foundation of Faith* (New York, NY: Philosophical Library, 1961), p. 69.

110. *Ibid.*, p. 71.

111. *Ibid.*, pp. 15-16. See Meland in *Creative Interchange*, ed. Broyer and Minor, p. 26: "Following a lecture at the University of Chicago several years after his retirement, Wieman was asked what would happen if human beings persisted in refusing to do the work which the growth of meaning requires." Wieman's reply: "Then the human species would disappear from the face of the planet, and the Creative Event would be thrown back upon less highly developed structures in nature. In that event the long, arduous process of creative emergence would begin all over again."

112. Wieman and Horton, *Growth of Religion*, p. 321.

113. *Ibid.*, p. 286.

114. Wieman, *Man's Ultimate Commitment*, p. 51.

115. See note 112.

116. Wieman, *Man's Ultimate Commitment*, p. 273.

117. Wieman, "Reply to Williams," in *Empirical Theology*, ed. Bretall, p. 102.

118. *Ibid.*

119. Wieman, "Reply to Pepper," in *Empirical Theology*, ed. Bretall, p. 163.

120. For additional discussion, see Mary Minella, "The Eschatological Dimension of Creative Interchange" in *Creative Interchange*, ed. Broyer and Minor, pp. 431-442.

121. Wieman, *Intellectual Foundation of Faith*, p. 158.

122. Wieman, *Creative Freedom*, p. 86.

123. Wieman, *The Wrestle of Religion with Truth*, p. 128.

124. *Ibid.*

125. *Ibid.*, p. 122.

126. *Ibid.*

127. *Ibid.*, p. 170.

128. Shuttee, "The Work of the Church," in *Empirical Theology*, ed. Bretall, p. 125.

129. Wieman and Horton, *The Growth of Religion*, p. 308.

130. Wieman with Regina Wescott Wieman, *Normative Psychology of Religion*, p. 225.

131. Wieman and Horton, *Growth of Religion*, p. 310.

132. Wieman, *Now We Must Choose* (New York, NY: Macmillan, 1941), p. 212.

133. Wieman, *The Source of Human Good*, p. 46.

134. *Ibid.*, p. 291.

135. *Ibid.*, pp. 42-43.

136. Wieman, *Man's Ultimate Commitment*, p. 165.

137. *Ibid.*, p. 132.

138. Wieman, *Religious Inquiry*, p. 135.

139. Wieman, *Creative Freedom*, p. 42.

140. Wieman, *Religious Inquiry*, pp. 135, 181.

141. Wieman, *Man's Ultimate Commitment*, p. 180.

Chapter Five: Critical Responses to Wieman's Thought

1. Wieman, *The Source of Human Good* (Chicago, IL: The University of Chicago Press, 1946), pp. 268-269.

2. Miller, *The American Spirit in Theology* (Philadelphia, PA: United Church Press, 1974), p. 176.

3. *Ibid.*, pp. 95-96.

4. Kuethe, "Three Empirical Philosophies of Religion:

Macintosh, Meland, and Wieman" (unpublished doctoral dissertation, Union Theological Seminary, New York, NY, 1963), p. 210.

5. Miller, *The American Spirit in Theology*, p. 138.

6. R. C. Miller, "Wieman's Theological Empiricism," in *The Empirical Theology of Henry Nelson Wieman*, ed. R. W. Bretall (Carbondale, IL: Southern Illinois University Press, 1963), p. 37.

7. J. Macquarrie, "The End of Empiricism," *Union Seminary Quarterly Review*, Fall/Winter 1981-1982, XXXVII (1 & 2): 61.

8. Nancy Frankenberry, *Religion and Radical Empiricism*, (Albany, NY: State University of New York Press, 1987), pp. 113-129.

9. *The Future of Empirical Theology,* ed. Bernard Meland (Chicago, IL: University of Chicago Press, 1969), pp. 35, 36.

10. J. A. Martin, *Empirical Philosophies of Religion with Special Reference to Boodin, Brightman, Hocking, Macintosh, and Wieman* (New York, NY: Columbia University Press, 1945), p. 106.

11. *Ibid.*, p. 99.

12. Miller, *The American Spirit in Theology*, pp. 96, 123.

13. Wieman, "Reply to Smith," in *Empirical Theology* ed. Bretall, p. 263.

14. Macquarrie, "The End of Empiricism," p. 65.

15. Quoted in Rosen, *Religious Education and Our Ultimate Commitment* (Lanham, MD: University Press of America, 1985), p. 92.

16. These issues are also taken up in Wieman *The Intellectual Foundation of Faith*, p. 105 ff.

17. William Dean, *American Religious Empiricism* (Albany, NY: State University of New York Press, 1986), p. 56, similarly finds fault with Charles Hartshorne.

Chapter Six: Wieman and Contemporary Theologies

1. Martin Luther King, Jr., *Strength to Love* (Philadelphia, PA: Fortress Press, 1981), copyright 1963.

2. Henry Nelson Wieman, *Religious Inquiry* (Boston, MA: Beacon Press, 1968), p. 155.

3. For further information about General Systems Theory, see Ludwig von Bertalanffy, *General Systems Theory* (New York, NY: Braziller, 1968) and E. Laszlo, *The Systems View of the World* (New York, NY: Braziller, 1972).

4. Freeman Dyson, *Infinite in All Directions* (New York, NY: Harper and Row, 1988), p. 298.

5. W. R. Miller, *The American Spirit in Theology* (Philadelphia, PA: United Church Press, 1974), p. 211.

6. Wieman and Bernard Meland, *American Philosophies of Religion* (Chicago, IL: Willet, Clark & Co., 1936), p. 345.

7. *Ibid.*, pp. 345-346.

8. Matthew Fox, *Original Blessing* (Santa Fe, NM: Bear & Company, 1983).

9. Wieman, *The Source of Human Good* (Chicago, IL: The University of Chicago Press, 1946), p. 155.

10. *Ibid.*, p. 144.

11. *Ibid.*, p. 147.

12. R. Mussard, "On Wieman's Philosophy of History," in *Creative Interchange*, ed. J. Broyer and W. Minor (Carbondale, IL: Southern Illinois University Press, 1982), p. 345 ff.

13. Stephen Pepper, "Wieman's Contextual Metaphysics," in *The Empirical Theology of Henry Nelson Wieman*, ed. R. W. Bretall (Carbondale, IL: Southern Illinois University Press, 1963), p. 151.

14. Wieman, *Methods of Private Religious Living* (New York, NY: Macmillan, 1929), p. 138.

15. R. M. Brown, *Creative Dislocation—The Movement of Grace* (Nashville, TN: Abingdon Press, 1980), pp. 141-142.

16. Carter Heyward, "Reflections on a Feminist Spirituality of Justice," in *Unitarian Universalism 1986: Se-*

lected Essays (Charlottesville, VA: Unitarian Universalist Ministers Association, 1986), p. 33.

17. C. Heyward, *Our Passion for Justice* (New York, NY: The Pilgrim Press, 1984), p. 29 ff.

18. *Ibid.*, p. 229.

19. See Wieman, *Man's Ultimate Commitment* (Carbondale, IL: Southern Illinois University Press, 1958), Chapt. 10, Industry, pp. 205-222. Also see Howard Parsons, "The Philosophies of Wieman and Marx Compared and Contrasted," in *Creative Interchange*, ed. Broyer and Minor, p. 361.

20. Wieman, *Man's Ultimate Commitment*, pp. 14-15.

21. Similarly, he would probably be troubled by C. Heyward's claim that "Those on the bottom—historically, those least empowered in the church and the world—are called by God to lead the way in discovering theological truths for our generation: theological truths and moral imperatives. It is not that women can speak for men. Or black people for whites. It is simply that poor people, people of darker shades and ethnic groups, women, lesbians and gay men, and members of religious minorities have what liberation theologians call an 'epistemological privilege'—the privilege of actually knowing God first, and therefore the ability to lead others to God." True enough, he would agree, "We speak our own theological truths" ("the heartbeat of feminist liberation theology," p. 34),

and God is present wherever justice arises. But, it is not the only place God can be known.

Chapter Seven: A Prophecy and a Song

1. See W. C. Roof and W. McKinney, *American Mainline Religion* (New Brunswick, NJ: Rutgers University Press, 1987), p. 214.

2. Daniel Day Williams, "Wieman as a Christian Theologian," in *The Empirical Theology of Henry Nelson Wieman,* ed. R. W. Bretall (Carbondale, IL: Southern Illinois University Press, 1963), pp. 95-96.

3. Daniel Day Williams, "Suffering and Being in Empirical Theology," in *The Future of Empirical Theology*, ed. Bernard Meland, (Chicago, IL: University of Chicago Press, 1969), p. 190.

4. *Ibid.*, p. 289.

5. Wieman, *The Source of Human Good* (Chicago, IL: The University of Chicago Press, 1946), p. 300.

6. Wieman, *Creative Freedom*, ed. Creighton Peden and Larry Axel (New York, NY: The Pilgrim Press, 1946), p. 68.

7. *Ibid.*, p. 45.

SELECTED BIBLIOGRAPHY

Books by Henry Nelson Wieman

Wieman, Henry Nelson, and Meland, Bernard. *American Philosophies of Religion*. Chicago, IL: Willet, Clark & Company, 1936.

_____. *Creative Freedom*. ed. C. Peden and L. Axel. New York, NY: The Pilgrim Press, 1982.

_____. *The Directive in History*. Boston, MA: Beacon Press, 1949.

_____, and Walter Marshall Horton. *The Growth of Religion*. Chicago, IL: Willet, Clark, 1938.

_____. *Intellectual Foundation of Faith*. New York, NY: Philosophical Library, 1961.

_____. *The Issues of Life*. New York, NY: Abingdon Press, 1930.

_____. *Man's Ultimate Commitment.* Carbondale, IL: Southern Illinois University Press, 1958.

_____. *Methods of Private Religious Living.* New York, NY: Macmillan, 1929.

_____, and Regina Westhall Wieman. *Normative Psychology of Religion.* New York, NY: Crowell, 1935.

_____. *Now We Must Choose.* New York, NY: Macmillan, 1941.

_____. *Religious Experience and Scientific Method.* New York, NY: Macmillan, 1926.

_____.*Religious Inquiry.* Boston, MA: Beacon Press, 1968.

_____. *Seeking a Faith for a New Age.* ed. Cedric Hepler. Metuchen, NJ: Scarecrow Press, 1975.

_____. *The Organization of Interests.* Lanham, MD: University Press of America, 1985. (Reprint of Wieman's dissertation.)

_____. *The Source of Human Good.* Chicago, IL: The University of Chicago Press, 1946.

_____. *The Wrestle of Religion with Truth.* New York, NY: Macmillan, 1927.

Articles by Henry Nelson Wieman

Wieman, Henry Nelson. "Authority and the Normative Approach." *Journal of Religion*, 1936, XVI: 175-202.

_____. "The Divine Creativity in History." *Religion in Life*, 1963, XXXIII(1): 52-65.

_____. "God, the Inescapable." *Christian Century*, 1931 XLVIII: 1170-1172, 1209-1211.

_____. "On Using Christian Words." *Journal of Religion* 1940, XX(3): 257-69.

_____. "Religious Humanism and Theism Rejected." *Religious Humanism*, 1968, II: 4.

_____. "Reply to My Critics." *Religion in Life*, 1963, XXXII(3): 454-70.

_____. "Salvation as Creative Evolution." *Religion in Life*, 1967, XXXVI(2): 191-201.

_____. "Science and a New Religious Reformation." *Zygon*, 1966, I(2): 125-39.

_____. "Some Blind Spots Removed." *Christian Century*, 1939, LVI: 116-118. Wieman's "Intellectual Autobiography" and sixteen replies to a variety of essays are included in Bretall, Robert W. *The Empirical Theology of Henry Nelson Wieman*. Carbondale, IL: Southern Illinois University Press, 1963.

Additional Resources

Ahlstrom, Sydney E. *A Religious History of the American People*. New Haven, CT: Yale University Press, 1972.

Bergland, James Wesley. "The Nature of Theological Inquiry in Henry Nelson Wieman." Unpublished Th.D. dissertation, Union Theological Seminary, 1972.

Bertalanffy, Ludwig. *General Systems Theory*. New York, NY: Braziller, 1968.

Bretall, R. W. ed. *The Empirical Theology of Henry Nelson Wieman*. Carbondale, IL: Southern Illinois University Press, 1963.

Broyer, J. and Minor, W. ed. *Creative Interchange*. Carbondale, IL: Southern Illinois University Press, 1982.

Brown, R. M. *Creative Dislocation—The Movement of Grace*. Nashville: Abingdon Press, 1980.

Burhoe, Ralph W. ed. *Science and Human Values in the 21st Century*. Philadelphia, PA: Westminster Press, 1971.

_____. *Toward A Scientific Theology*. Belfast, Ireland: Christian Journals Limited, 1981.

Calvin, John. *Institutes of the Christian Religion*. Translated by Henry Beveridge. Grand Rapids: Eerdmans, 1972.

Cauthen, Kenneth, *The Impact of American Liberalism*. New York, NY: Harper and Row, 1961.

Conlan, F. Allan. *A Critique of the Philosophy of Religion of Henry Nelson Wieman in the Light of Thomistic Principles*. Washington, DC: The Catholic University of America Press, 1958.

Cousins, Ewert, ed. *Process Theology: Basic Writings*. New York, NY: Newman Press, 1971.

Dean, William. *American Religious Empiricism*. Albany, NY: State University of New York Press, 1986.

Dyson, Freeman. *Infinite In All Directions*. New York, NY: Harper and Row, 1988.

Edgerton, Glenn S., Jr. "Authority, Reason and Experience: An Essay on the Role of Philosophical Presuppositions in Theological Method in American Protestant Theology: 1929-1946." Unpublished Ph.D. dissertation, Columbia University, 1971.

Farley, W. E. "The Most High: A Study of the Doctrine of Transcendence of God in Contemporary Philosophical Theology." Unpublished Ph.D. dissertation, Columbia University, 1958.

Fox, Matthew. *Compassion*. Minneapolis, MN: Winston Press, 1979.

_____. *Original Blessing*. Santa Fe, NM: Bear and Company, 1983.

_____. *The Cosmic Christ*. San Francisco, CA: Harper and Row, 1988.

Frankenberry, Nancy. *Religion and Radical Empiricism*. Albany, NY: State University of New York Press, 1987.

Harrington, Donald Szantho. *Outstretched Wings of the Spirit—A Lenten Manual Based on the Theology of Henry Nelson Wieman and Regina Westcott Wieman*. Boston, MA: Unitarian Universalist Association, 1980.

Heyward, Carter. *Our Passion for Justice*. New York, NY: The Pilgrim Press, 1984.

_____. *The Redemption of God*. Washington, DC: University Press of America, 1982.

_____. "Reflections on a Spirituality of Justice," in *Unitarian Universalism 1986: Selected Essays*. Charlottesville, VA: Unitarian Universalist Ministers Association, 1986.

_____. *Touching Our Strength*. San Francisco, CA: Harper and Row, 1989.

Kuethe, J. "Three Empirical Philosophies of Religion: Macintosh, Meland, and Wieman." Unpublished Ph.D. dissertation, Columbia University, 1963.

Laszlo, Ervin. *The Systems View of the World*. New York, NY: Braziller, 1972.

Lovelock, J. *The Ages of Gaia*. New York, NY: W. W. Norton and Company, 1988.

_____. *Gaia*. Oxford, England: Oxford University Press, 1979.

Macquarrie, J. *Twentieth Century Religious Thought*. New York, NY: Charles Scribner's Sons, 1981, revised edition.

Martin, J.A. *Empirical Philosophies of Religion with Special Reference to Boodin, Brightman, Hocking, Macintosh, and Wieman*. New York, NY: Columbia University Press, 1945.

Meland, Bernard, ed. *The Future of Empirical Theology*. Chicago, IL: University of Chicago Press, 1969.

Miller, Randolph Crump. *The American Spirit in Theology*. Philadelphia, PA: United Church Press, 1974.

Miller, William. *Contemporary American Protestant Thought: 1900-1970*. Indianapolis, IN: Bobbs-Merrill Company, Inc., 1973.

Miller, William, ed. *Empirical Theology—A Handbook*. Birmingham, AL: Religious Education Press, 1992.

Minor, W. *Creativity in Henry Nelson Wieman*. Metuchen, NJ: Scarecrow Press, 1977.

Mosala, Itumeleng. *Biblical Hermeneutics and Black Theology*. Grand Rapids, MI: William B. Eerdmans Publishing Company, 1989.

"Naturalism and Theism," *Zygon*. Vol. 22, No. 1, March, 1987.

Peden, C. and Axel, L. *God, Values and Empiricism: Issues in Philosophical Theology*. Macon, GA: Mercer University Press, 1989.

Pepper, Stephen. *World Hypotheses: A Study in Evidence*. Berkeley, CA: University of California Press, 1948.

Roof, W. C. and McKinney, W. *American Mainline Religion*. New Brunswick, NJ: Rutgers University Press, 1987.

Rosen, H. *Religious Education and Our Ultimate Commitment*. Lanham, MD: University Press of America, 1985.

Shaw, Marvin. "Naturalism and the Christ: Wieman's Christology." unpublished manuscript.

Soelle, D. *The Strength of the Weak*. Philadelphia, PA: The Westminister Press, 1984.

_____. *To Work and to Love*. Philadelphia, PA: The Fortress Press, 1984.

Sullivan, Harry Stack. *The Interpersonal Theory of Psychiatry*. New York, NY: W.W. Norton & Co., 1953.

Terry, Franklin. "The Problem of Evil and the Promise of Hope in the Theology of Henry Nelson Wieman." *Religion in Life*, 1970, XXXIX(4): 582-594.

Tillich, Paul. *Systematic Theology*. Chicago, IL: University of Chicago Press. Vol. I, 1951; II, 1957; III, 1963.

Waller, J. ed. "Essays in Honor of James A. Martin, Jr." *Union Seminary Quarterly Review*, 1981-1982, XXXVII, (1 & 2).

West, Cornel. *Prophesy Deliverance*. Philadelphia, PA: Westminister Press, 1982.

_____. *The American Evasion of Philosophy: A Genealogy of Pragmatism*. Madison, WI: The University of Wisconsin Press, 1989.

Whitehead, Alfred North. *Process and Reality*. New York, NY: Macmillan, 1926.

_____. *Religion in the Making*. New York, NY: Macmillan, 1929.

Williams, Daniel Day. *The Spirit and Forms of Love*. New York, NY: Harper and Row, 1968.

_____. *What Present Day Theologians are Thinking*. Revised third edition. New York, NY: Harper and Row, 1967.

INDEX